Praise for:

The College to Career Road Map: A Four-Year Guide to Coaching Your Student

"Going to college is more important, more expensive, and more challenging than ever. Students take longer than in the past to get their "four-year" degree—if they get it at all—in part because they know too little about how to navigate their way toward that goal. This book provides an excellent guide to a successful college experience. By describing in detail the "What," "Why," and "How" of each year of a four-year college education, along with specific activities that encourage discussion and reflection, the book provides advice and information that students and their parents will find highly valuable."

JEFFREY JENSEN ARNETT
Author of *Emerging Adulthood: The Winding Road from the Late Teens Through the Twenties* (Oxford University Press, 2004)
www.jeffreyarnett.com

"*The College to Career Road Map* is a thoughtful, thorough, and exceptionally useful book. Parents will return to it again and again as they coach their college-age children on the road to independence. While it's written for parents, the authors never forget that the journey belongs to the students."

KAREN LEVIN COBURN
Co-author of *Letting Go: A Parent's Guide to Understanding the College Years* (HarperCollins, 2003)
www.lettinggobook.com

"This book touches on all of the key aspects of helping students make that sometimes difficult transition from school to the world of work (or graduate school). The Road Map is especially fine, but the book does so much more than that. Its tone and focus is to encourage parents to support their students in reflecting on their unique passions, talents, and values. That approach is sorely needed for this generation of young people, who are so 'connected' and pushed to achieve that they rarely have the time (nor are they encouraged) to delve deeper in uncovering a meaningful, individual path in life."

HELEN E. JOHNSON
Co-author of *Don't Tell Me What to Do, Just Send Money:*
The Essential Parenting Guide to the College Years (St. Martin's Press, 2000)
www.collegeparentsaspartners.com

"Choosing a career is frequently mystifying for students and misunderstood by parents. Most families either urge their student to choose a career with a guaranteed good income or they trust the outcome to fate. *The College to Career Road Map* traces a route that honors the student, builds family ties, and will yield not just a job but a life path."

MARJORIE SAVAGE
Author of *You're on Your Own (but I'm Here If You Need Me):*
Mentoring Your Child During the College Years (Fireside, 2003)
www.parent.umn.edu

"Parents need to wear many different hats, including that of career coach. This book gives you everything you'd ever need to make that hat fit."

ROBIN RASKIN
Author of *Parents' Guide to College Life: Straight Answers on Everything*
You Can Expect Over the Next Four Years (Random House, 2006)
www.robinraskin.com

"Filled with gems, wisdom, and insights to help college students navigate the transition from college to a life driven by purpose! Brilliant thinking in a most creative format."

RICH FELLER
Author of *Knowledge Nomads and the Nervously Employed:*
Workplace Change & Courageous Career Choices (Pro-Ed, 2005)
soe.cahs.colostate.edu/faculty/feller

"*The College to Career Road Map* is a must for today's parents who wish to help their students become productive and successful in college without *hovering* over them. The authors tactfully help parents use their life experiences, and then get them close enough to coach and help optimize their students' decision making. Do not send your student to college before reading this book."

WILLIAM KROCAK
Founder and President of MindSight Assessment Products, Inc.
www.mindsightinc.com

the

COLLEGE

to

CAREER

ROAD MAP

a four-year guide to
coaching your student

•PARENT EDITION•

TERESE COREY BLANCK, PETER VOGT
and JUDITH ANDERSON

Atwood Publishing • Madison, WI

The College to Career Road Map: A Four-Year Guide to Coaching Your Student
by Terese Corey Blanck, Peter Vogt, and Judith Anderson

Copyright © 2006
Atwood Publishing
Madison, WI 53704

Cover and text design © TLC Graphics, *www.TLCGraphics.com*

Library of Congress Cataloging-in-Publication Data

Blanck, Terese Corey, 1961-

  The college to career road map : a four-year guide to coaching your
student / by Terese Corey Blanck, Peter Vogt, and Judith Anderson. —
Parent ed.
      p. cm.
  Companion to: The college to career road map : a four-year guide to
finding your path.
  ISBN-13: 978-1-891859-65-6 (pbk.)
  1. College majors—United States. 2. College students—Vocational
guidance—United States. 3. Education, Higher—Parent
participation—United States. 4. Career development—United States. I.
Vogt, Peter, 1967- II. Anderson, Judith, 1971- III. Title.

  LB2361.5.B575 2006
  378.1'98--dc22

                              2006025878

the

COLLEGE

to

CAREER

ROAD MAP

a four-year guide to
coaching your student

Foreword

Remember how you felt the first time you stood on the soccer sideline, or in the auditorium at the band concert, and your child was about to perform, for the very first time, before you and your fellow parents?

There were probably some butterflies in your stomach. You wanted so desperately for your child to succeed that perhaps you had to stop from running out on the field or up on the stage to kick that ball or play that trumpet yourself. Somehow you held back, yelled out words of encouragement, and it all worked out in the end.

Now your child is about to "perform" again, this time for keeps. He or she is embarking on or taking significant new steps along a college and career journey. You are smarter now and you realize that, in the end, your child must make the most of his or her own college and career opportunities.

But you still want to help, as you should. And no doubt that is why you have picked up this copy of *The College to Career Road Map: A Four-Year*

Guide to Coaching Your Student. Congratulations. You realize that empowering yourself to best support your child on the road to college graduation, and beyond, is not only an effort of a loving heart, but also of a wiser head.

Our national organization, College Parents of America, is all about parent empowerment. Our mission is to support parents with children in the middle school years, all the way until those children are ready to enroll in graduate school or join the workforce. We look for "best-in-class" resources in every field, and there is no team of authors better in class than Terese Corey Blanck, Peter Vogt, and Judy Anderson.

Enjoy, and benefit from, their collective forty-plus years of wisdom working with students, hiring managers, and the world's most well-known Internet job site.

~ JIM BOYLE • 2006
President
College Parents of America
www.collegeparents.org

Acknowledgments

The three of us would like to collectively thank all the people who have contributed to the process of developing this book in some way, shape, or form.

First, our gratitude goes to Marjorie Savage—author of *You're on Your Own (but I'm Here If You Need Me): Mentoring Your Child During the College Years* (Fireside, 2003) and director of the University of Minnesota Parent Program—who provided us with instrumental feedback and ideas regarding publishing. Her willingness to answer questions along the way has been essential to our learning process.

Our thanks to those who reviewed early drafts of the book. Among them are Scott Simpson and Kimberly Strauss-Johnson, who both reviewed the book in its early stages from a career development perspective. We would also like to thank several other early reviewers whose comments helped shape the content of the book: Bethany (senior at The College of St. Catherine), Brent (sophomore at St. John's University), and Lisa Fenhaus (parent);

Cindy Nelson (parent); Beth Feine; and Kathy Frost. Thanks as well to Gretchen Helmer for additional thoughts on wording and phrasing.

We also greatly appreciate the efforts and insights of our prepublication reviewers: Jeffrey Arnett, Janis Brody, Karen Levin Coburn, Rich Feller, Allison Hemming, Helen Johnson, Bill Krocak, Alexandra Levit, Robin Raskin, and Stephen Viscusi. Additionally, we'd like to thank Steven Rothberg and Jim Boyle for graciously writing the forewords for each of *The College to Career Road Map* books.

Another thank you to our spouses, who by proximity were called upon for their individual talent and expertise: Russell Blanck for his legal counsel and wording and phrasing advice; Lois Vogt for her willingness to do any and all research and administrative work; and Scott Anderson for his business perspective and technical assistance.

Finally, our heartfelt gratitude goes to Linda Babler, for seeing the value of offering parents and students a companion set of books. This approach goes beyond the normal bounds of the publishing industry. Thanks too to our editor, William Cody, who polished our words and made sure we were consistent. Additionally, Tami Dever and Erin Stark of TLC Graphics have been incredibly responsive to our ideas about the feel of the books, which was very important to us. Tami and Erin, your design has added a new dimension to the books and was a fun process to participate in—a tremendous bonus as far as we're concerned. To all three of you—thanks for bringing our books to life!

My gratitude goes out to all those who have inspired me to find "what matters most" throughout my life. I can't imagine writing this book without the morsels of wisdom I received from those I met along the way.

Although high school wasn't the place I pondered my life path or even career, I must thank John Hegg for directing me to college. When I arrived at MSU Mankato's campus, my life's path began to take form. I met Arnie Oudenhoven, Sue Bartolutti, Tony Mueller—who always knew what I was going to say before I said it—and, in particular, Malcolm O'Sullivan. All of you shared with me the beauty of the "student affairs" profession, guiding students through the maze of the college experience.

I couldn't have wished for a more enlightening graduate learning experience than the one I found at Colorado State University. The insightful people there inspired me to question not less than everything I knew to be true. Dr. James Kuder, Dr. Dave McKelfresh, Rich Feller, and my classmates all challenged me to ponder the "big questions." Anne Williams Hudgens, I will never forget the horseback ride in the mountains above Boulder, where we pondered life and living intentionally. Your coaching touched my life and added meaning.

This book would never have happened without the love and support of my family and friends. My siblings, parents, grandparents, and Aunt Beverley provided the subtle nuances of family dynamics that played a vital role in nurturing out my true self. Mother, you generously partnered with me throughout my two years of writing. You have been my single most positive supporter. Thank you … your spirit is always welcome! I must mention my mother's dear friends in Canton, South Dakota, who were so much a part of anything good that became the children who've grown up there. I was fortunate enough to be one of them.

My heartfelt gratitude to the coffee shop crew: Caroline and Kelly, you always start my day right; and Jane … your enthusiasm and continued interest has been such great support … it was a pleasure to be greeted every time with genuine kindness! Thank you to Dr. Dave, Jeanine, and the LADC boys for listening to my updates. Lillian, you asked about the book every time I saw you and brought a smile to my face. Judy and Candace, you kept me balanced … thanks! My friends from the "Village," especially Tom and Jamie, thank you for asking and showing your excitement along my journey. Susan Ralles, without your question about how I knew all this college "stuff," … the parent book would never have been born … thank you. Clay, my kindred spirit in writing, your support of this project as well as your friendship over twenty years has been a true gem.

Learning how to be intentional parents is the specific purpose of this book. Yet, one need not be a parent to make an indelible impact upon a college student, and I am a case in point. The many mentors, advisors, parents, friends, and family members I've been blessed to know along the way helped me find the path that resonated with me. My gratitude goes out to those who remain unnamed who served as mentors, guides, or friends.

A special tribute goes to my two partners, Peter and Judy, who've logged many hours with me, writing, laughing, and enjoying life!

I owe my deepest appreciation and gratitude to my husband. While I wrote this book with my co-authors, he bestowed upon me (us) his patience, humor, legal counsel, perspective, and interest. The courage he displayed in radically diverting from his own "pre-determined" career path is the fodder upon which this book is based! Your support of the book from conception has meant so much to me. Your belief in my work has been my strength. You are my true companion.

Last but not least, I dedicate this book to my lovely daughter, Alexandra Rachel Talia Corey Blanck, who inspires me to think about life and the tender parent–child connection that can let loose the possibilities of finding one's own soul. You are my teacher. I love you with all my heart. May you find the path that fits you throughout your life and may the journey be sweet.

~ Terese Corey Blanck

Any book you pick up is *much* more than its authors—and this book is no different.

I'd like to first thank my colleagues and co-authors, Terese Corey Blanck and Judy Anderson. Terese, I appreciate your visionary ideas and your passion. Judy, I appreciate your thoroughness and—especially—your closing abilities; *The College to Career Road Map* wouldn't exist without you.

Thanks as well to Linda Babler, publisher and president of Atwood Publishing. Linda, thanks for believing in both the concepts and the people behind *The College to Career Road Map*.

Thanks to my parents, Charles and Nancy Vogt, and my siblings—Kathy Frost, Mike Vogt, and Mark Vogt—and their families, who all have supported me in whatever I do. Thanks as well to my parents-in-law, Marilyn and the late Merv Gessele.

Many movie credits list the characters in order of their appearance in the film. My mind works that way when it comes to thanking people for their contributions to a book like this one. So from here on out, I'll start from the very beginning and work my way to the present. Here goes …

To my high school English instructor, Mark Hassenstab—I'm sorry for hassling you so much (it was the other boys' fault), but I appreciate your hanging in there with me and teaching me something about how to write. I still don't know why you never killed me or my partners in crime; thanks for your restraint.

To my Moorhead State University instructors Melva Moline and the late Joe Dill—thanks for teaching me to think before I write. And to Shelton Gunaratne—you drove me and my fellow students nuts with your nit-pickiness; but upon reflection, I can only thank you for refusing to lower your high standards. I now know that the power of the written word was at stake.

To my old colleagues at *The Forum* in Fargo, North Dakota—especially Mark Hvidsten (the guy who taught me the day-to-day ropes) and Dennis Doeden (the guy who hired me). I may not have become a sportswriter, but that doesn't mean I didn't learn a lot from you.

To my colleagues at Magna Publications in Madison, Wisconsin—Mary Lou Santovec, Charles Bryan, Doris Green, Robert Magnan, Linda Babler, and Marilyn Annucci. I appreciate your taking a chance on a fresh-grad rookie. And to you especially, Bob—thanks for teaching me how to actually think, whether it was over my keyboard or sitting across from you at Rocky Rococo.

To my graduate school professors at the University of Wisconsin–Whitewater, especially Anene Okocha. Anene, I appreciate all you taught me, not only about career development but also about research. Brenda O'Beirne, you modeled what it was like to be passionate about one's career—something I had honestly never seen before—and Steven Friedman, you made the idea of conducting research somehow appealing. Thanks to all three of you for the expertise you lent during the challenging journey that is called the master's thesis.

To my colleagues and mentors at the University of Wisconsin–Whitewater Office of Career Services—Gail Fox, Carolyn Gorby, Jerry McDonald, and Kathy Craney—as well as Marge O'Leary, Eunice Lehner, Margaret Pelischek, and Kris Fantetti. How can I ever thank you all enough for what you taught me about the field of career services? Gail, a very special thank-you to you—not only for inviting me into the field of career development but also encouraging me to stick around for a while. There's a book out there called *The Five People You Meet in Heaven*, which suggests that when you get to heaven you'll be met by the five people in your life who had the most impact on you. I'm certain, Gail, that you'll be one of the five where my life is concerned.

To my colleagues and mentors at Edgewood College Career & Counseling Services—George Heideman, Shawn Johnson Williams, Janet Billerbeck, Merle Bailey, Sharon Boeder, Rose White, and Julie Bonk. I couldn't have been more welcomed or more blessed. George and Shawn, special thanks to both of you for not only teaching me about career issues, but helping me understand that I had knowledge and skills to contribute too. Thanks as well to several other Edgewood colleagues and friends who taught me so much: Jan Zimmerman, Maggie Balistreri-Clarke, Maureen McDonnell, Todd Benson, and Debora Barrera-Pontillo.

I highly value my connection with the good folks at Monster and MonsterTRAK! Thanks in particular to the fabulous content producers I've worked with over the years: Denis Gaynor, David Long, Kristy Meghreblian, Christina Lopez, Christine Stavrou, Ryck Lent, Christine DellaMonaca, Ann Pariani, Norma Mushkat Gaffin, and Thad Peterson.

Special thanks to Barbara Winter as well. Barbara, I'll never forget the key piece of wisdom you shared with me over coffee a while back: "Writing, Peter, involves putting words on paper!"

Last but certainly not least, thanks to my wife Lois (for your patience even when you didn't always know what I was up to!) and my son Isaac (for letting me write even when you didn't always want me to). What would I do without my wonderful family? You're the reason I do what I do.

~ Peter Vogt

Many authors will say that writing a book is truly a journey—and this journey started long ago as I discovered my passion.

I'd first like to thank my partners, Terese Corey Blanck and Peter Vogt, who accepted the challenge of co-writing with open hearts and minds. I am truly amazed at how well each of our talents blended together to produce a book that will impact so many college students.

Thanks as well to my parents, Carol and Bill Roche, and my siblings—Nancy, Sandra (Nick), Stephen (Kristin), Charlie, and Helen—who will always be a part of my life. My in-laws, Jonette and Terry Anderson, and my sister-in-law Christi (Matt) also deserve a thank you for their love and support.

My thanks to Phil Fishman, adjunct professor at the University of Minnesota—who invited our class out for coffee and offered his interest and advice. This made a big difference to me. He guided me through the graduate school decision-making process and always takes my phone call at his law office. Terese Corey Blanck (yes, the same one) also spent many hours talking, teaching, and questioning during my four years in Comstock Hall. She too deserves much credit and thanks for introducing me to my career.

I also need to thank Orientation Services at the University of Iowa for shaping my entire graduate school experience. I was given a unique chance to be in a position of responsibility during my second year of graduate school. I want to thank Tom DePrenger, Jan Warren, Cathy Solow, Emil Rinderspacher, and Marilyn Kempnich for believing I could do the job. I also want to thank Cassidy Titcomb, Steve Hubbard, Dave Borgealt, and Laurie DuFoe for sharing all of what we learned during graduate school. I learned to expect more from college students than they expected from themselves and to share in their satisfaction when they reached those expectations.

I also want to thank Carmela Kranz, Elizabeth Patty, Karla Hoff, Libby Tate, and the late Deanna Hamilton for what they taught me at the University of Minnesota Alumni Association—and for the fun! The mentor program coordinators and alumni volunteers are too many to name—but you know how important the University of Minnesota Mentor Connection was to me. The Student Alumni Leaders were more than just a student group—I thank each of them for sharing their stories with me.

I also want to thank Laura Coffin Koch and LeeAnn Melin, who have been my mentors and friends—your wisdom and advice means a lot to me.

I want to thank my husband (and best friend), Scott, who has been completely supportive during this process. He has never questioned why I have the need or passion to make a difference—he only supports it. I dedicate this book to my children, Maxwell, Madeline, and Jack, who make me laugh every day as they truly explore their talents, passions, and values as only little children can do. It's amazing to watch each of your personalities take shape and to dream the dream of your future! Each one of you is special and will find your passion as only you can.

~ *Judith Anderson*

• PARENT GUIDE •

Table of Contents

—◦—

━━◦━━

Introduction

The College to Career Road Map and this *Companion Parent Guide* offer you and your college student a rare opportunity: The chance to engage in illuminating career dialogue throughout your student's four (or more) college years. Our goal in these innovative books is simple: to provide the detailed road map your student needs to find a satisfying career—one that aligns with his purpose and pays the bills!

The *Parent Guide* will help you guide your student through the ever-complex career development process by allowing you to take on the role of career coach. Like an athletic coach, you don't have all the answers, nor should you. Instead, your task is to help your student help himself using *The College to Career Road Map* as his handbook. The *Road Map* outlines the career-building activities that are most critical for your student to work on during the college years. Its focus is on both the *academic* and the *experiential* activities that will help your student discern his future direction and boost his chances of landing a fulfilling job after graduation.

Here's what's most unique about *The College to Career Road Map*: Each activity we've outlined tells students not only *what* they need to do, but also *why* the task is so important and *how* students can actually go about completing that task. (Most career resources focus solely on the what and foolishly overlook the why and the how—both of which are critical in the minds of today's savvy college students.) Additionally, each activity is explicitly tied to the three most important aspects of career decision making where college students and recent graduates are concerned:

- Finding one's *passions*.
- Uncovering one's *innate talents*.
- Determining *what matters most* (i.e., one's values) in work and in life.

The *Road Map* is grounded in the philosophy that, while the career activities we've outlined are important in their own right, much more valuable are the reflection and discussion that help students learn about themselves and then apply that critical knowledge to their future career decisions.

This *Parent Guide* is meant to be a *facilitative* guide, not an *instructional* one. We believe that every person is unique, and that every person has the potential to be successful and satisfied (in whatever form that takes for him/her). We begin with the belief that the process of *facilitating* is a fluid and flexible one that is designed to help your student step back and see who he is now and who he is becoming. It's a personalized development process that enables your student to experience the impact of his actions (and, in some cases, inactions). It's designed to help you discuss these discoveries with your student in an exploratory, safe manner in which you're focused on *facilitating*—not *telling* or *instructing* or *expecting*.

Your primary role as a parent coach is to help your student uncover the hidden blocks and issues facing him head-on as he ponders the wide world of careers. Think of it this way: You're helping your student remove barriers so he can see possibilities. If you can do that in a naturally comfortable way—one that feels caring and non-judgmental to your student—you'll form a new bond with him and create a new aspect to your relationship that will serve both of you well throughout the rest of your lives. (Note: Keep in mind that *The College to Career Road Map* and this *Parent Guide* outline a process your student can complete with you or with another trusted adult. What matters is that your student has someone he can go to for support in the career decision-making process.)

The *Parent Guide* offers specific exercises aimed at each year of college: freshman, sophomore, junior, and senior. Ideally, you and your student will complete these exercises together to get your conversations going, but in some cases you may need to adapt the main principle(s) behind a particular exercise and talk to your student your *own* way. Know that either approach is effective.

We've also embedded some helpful tips on facilitating each exercise with your student. We want you to get beyond the common "I don't know" type of response your student may put forth—the one that merely frustrates both of you. Ninety percent of the time, college students really don't know the answers to the difficult life questions they face as they attempt to find their direction. It *is* a challenging journey for them. You can help best, then, by *gently* probing, guiding, and—most importantly—listening.

Remember: This is truly a learning situation for both you and your student. In the process of choosing a career, your student needs to find the doorway to who he is—in all respects—and experience success while he's developing a new and unique relationship with you.

The Parent Coaching Model

One of the primary challenges you face as the parent of a college student is that you've been a parent for at least eighteen years or so! The parental habits that have kept your child safe and happy for nearly two decades can now start to work against you in some ways as your emerging-adult student begins seriously exploring career options and "The Future."

That's why the *Parent Coaching* model focuses on helping you acknowledge this pending change and open yourself up to a new kind of parenting experience. Sometimes that experience will feel unnatural and out of your control. That's completely normal. And if you think about it, you already know deep down that your student needs to develop her own thoughts and feelings about the future. All college students must discover who they are and where they want to go in life. Indeed, that's essentially what college is all about.

With that in mind, we outline below five core principles for being an effective facilitator, or career *coach*, for your college student. Remember: You'll be going through at least a four-year process. Some of your conversations with your student will go fabulously; others will leave you feeling empty and confused, and possibly even frustrated with your student's motivations, decisions, and general direction. It's all par for the course. What matters is that you're taking an active role in opening up a line of career dialogue with your student. You'll thus be more apt to experience (or at least hear about!) her successes, her joys, her discoveries, and her passions—and ultimately, you'll get to know your student on a much more intimate and trusting level than ever before.

The Five Core Principles of the Parent Coaching Model

Listen for Understanding

The College to Career Road Map and this *Parent Guide* will compel your student to dive into a profound mode of introspection about his life and his life's purpose. The questions posed throughout both books will help your student start to reflect on what's meaningful to him and learn how to integrate those reflections into the choices he's making along his college and career journey.

In the meantime, you—as the parent coach—will be *listening* to your student process and struggle with these difficult questions. Deeper conversations will naturally emerge, and that's when your listening skills will play a vital role. Your student will be rolling around choices he's contemplating and looking for your reactions and sometimes even your "answers." Be careful! Your student needs to find his *own* answers. So *listen* to your student grapple with the questions.

Your student has entered the gray zone of life, where he must dig much deeper to find the answers that will enrich his life with purpose. Up until this point, your student has probably viewed the world in black-and-white terms. Now, he's in the midst of a developmental process that challenges him to view the world through different lenses—gray ones—and shed the simplicity of seeing the world concretely.

The beauty of simply listening to your student—and avoiding the common temptation to offer "answers"—is that you'll give your student the chance to live with all of these questions and think about them ... on the way to class, in the shower, in the car. At some point, your student will have an "aha" moment and an answer will begin to crystallize. It may happen when the two of you are sitting together talking, or it may happen during a phone conversation when suddenly the light goes on and your student realizes the answer is right in front of him—and then he shares it with you!

Throughout your student's career exploration and decision-making activities, clear your mind and hold on to those well-meaning pieces of wisdom you so desperately want to share with your student when you're chatting with him about careers. Just listen and ask questions that will help him go further into his discovery process. You'll be amazed at what you hear.

• LESSONS ON LISTENING •

Listening is not like breathing. *Listening doesn't come naturally to most people. But it is a skill you can learn through practice.*

Your listening style has a history. *How well (or poorly) you listen is directly connected to your family upbringing. Do you frequently interrupt others when they're talking? Do you half-listen so you can think about what you're going to say in response? Observe your family of origin the next time you have a chance and see how you were taught to listen. Do you have any work to do where your listening—and thus coaching—skills are concerned?*

Listening is one of the cornerstones of effective coaching. *Let your student know she can (and should) give you feedback as the two of you work together on career activities. (Note: Be prepared to feel a little awkward the first time your student gives you feedback on your listening skills. You may feel a bit defensive. But it's critical for you to understand what works best for your student when it comes to discussing her career issues with you.)*

Beware of the blocks to good listening. *Common blocks like these will impair your ability to listen to your student effectively:*

- **Lack of time.** *Make sure you're not rushed during the conversations you have with your student. If at all possible, set aside specific time to chat with her, either in person or on the phone. Don't try to cover too much territory. Instead, let your student bring to you what's most pressing to her at the time.*

- **A busy mind.** *We all wrestle with "inside chatter" in our minds. But if you're going to be fully present as a listener, you need to quiet your thoughts and focus on your student.*

- **Unruly emotions.** *Clear any emotions that may get in the way of your listening: fear, anger, worry, and the like.*

Question to Uncover Ideas

By simply asking good questions, you'll help your student identify his innate talents—not to mention his attitudes, behaviors, and passions—which in turn will help him uncover his potential and explore ways to fulfill that potential via his career.

All great coaches are skilled questioners. You can become one too. If you're someone who has unquenchable curiosity to begin with, then you may already have this essential ability. Even if you're not a naturally inquisitive person, though, you can still ask questions that will give you an honest, inside view of all that's happening in the recesses of your student's mind, heart, and soul.

Here are a few types of questions you can ask, ranging from the most basic to the most complex:

- *Knowledge/comprehension questions.* Ask questions to determine if your student understands something. For example: "How would you describe _____ ?" or "How would you show _____ ?" Does your student have the knowledge he needs to make key decisions or support his assumptions?

- *Application questions.* Can your student see how one piece of knowledge or information relates to another? For example: "What approach would you use if _____ ?" or "What would happen if _____ ?" or "What would you do if _____ ?" Has your student digested his knowledge in a way that will help him make connections and expand his career possibilities?

- *Analytical/evaluative questions.* These are the types of questions that will help your student defend an opinion or break a complex concept down into smaller parts. Examples: "What could you do to improve _____ ?" or "What proof can you find of _____ ?"

- *Assumption-challenging questions.* "How do you know _____ is true?" "What data do you have to support your assumption that _____ ?" If your student, like many, is drawing conclusions based on poor or even nonexistent data, then he might well fail to explore a potentially enriching career. That would be a tragedy. So when your student tells you, for instance, that he loves writing but that he "could never make a living at it," challenge that assumption. How does he know he could never make a living using his writing skills? Where did that conclusion come from?

Promote Action

Ultimately, the career discussions you have with your student must lead to action on her part—even if she feels she doesn't have every piece of information she needs to make a decision and move forward. It's a daunting prospect to be sure, so don't be shocked if your student seems stuck at times. Your job is to help her get unstuck.

Suppose, for example, that your student knows she needs to get some work experience but she's been hesitant to take the steps necessary to find an internship, a part-time job, or even a volunteer opportunity. You can help her get moving by showing her how to break the task down into manageable pieces. You could encourage her to take these steps:

1. Search the school's web site for the campus career center's site.

2. Call the career center and set up an appointment with a career counselor there to learn about various ways to obtain relevant work experience.

3. Write down a few questions in preparation for the appointment, in order to review past experiences and skills gained.

4. Attend the appointment.

5. Follow up on whatever actions are necessary to take action based on the counseling session.

• HELP YOUR STUDENT GET UNSTUCK •

We all get stuck at certain points in our lives, especially where our careers are concerned. If your student is stuck during some part of the career journey, here's how you can help—and not harm:

- **Be gentle and supportive.** *Don't criticize your student for his confusion or tell him you're disappointed in him.*

- **Let go of blame.** *You may feel responsible for your student's inaction. You might even feel it reflects badly on your parenting when all it really means is that your student is stuck at the moment. That's neither good nor bad; it just is what it is. There's no blame to be meted out to anyone.*

- **Seek to understand.** *Ask your student what he says he wants to do that he has (so far) failed to do. All it takes is a simple question.*

For example:

Help me understand how important this is to you. Last time we talked you said you needed to look into getting experience, but nothing has happened yet. Do you need to change this goal or maybe go about it in a different way?

- **Break things down.** *Your student might look at the task(s) ahead as being too "big" to even start, let alone accomplish. So help him break the task down into smaller, more manageable pieces that he can complete—one by one—to achieve his goal.*

Engage in Dialogue

Talk to your student about her ongoing discoveries and the career possibilities those discoveries present. Granted, technology has changed the way we communicate with our young-adult sons and daughters (and everyone else!). Indeed, most of today's emerging adults are used to developing and carrying on entire relationships via short text messages. But that doesn't mean your student isn't interested in discussing her future with you—in depth. Yes, it may take some time for her quick sound bytes and surface-level responses to transform into deeper conversations with you. Then again, she may be hungry to be heard and taken seriously by an adult who cares deeply about her.

You'll find out soon enough where her comfort level is. Meet her there, and use the elements of solid communication to talk with her, not at her. Make sure she knows she's the center of your attention. Listen non-judgmentally and reflect back what she's saying so she knows you understand. And look for nonverbal signs—facial expressions, posture, etc.—that offer clues as to the real meaning behind her words.

• 8 WAYS TO BE A MINDFUL CAREER COACH •

Mindfulness is the ability to allow your mind to be open and uncluttered, clear of the barriers of stress, worry, and preconceived notions that will prevent you from helping your student fully explore her career possibilities. When you work with your student, start with an open mind—one that is mindful of keeping your internal voices at bay.

Your goal is to be completely present for your student. Here's how:

- Spend 90% of your time listening and 10% talking—with 90% of your talking time asking questions and 10% of it making statements.

- Ask questions to help your student clarify her thinking.

- Engage in dialogue that is transformational—the kind that helps your student discover something she really didn't know or consider before.

- Allow new ideas to emerge in your student's mind. (Don't poo-poo something you think is ridiculous at first glance.)

- Understand that the learning moment will occur when distractions fall away and your student's own innate knowing appears. Such personal insights will change your student's thoughts and beliefs—and, therefore, her future. The possibilities now begin to take shape!

- Focus on your student's potential from the inside out. Don't focus *solely on what you can "see." Examine what you don't see or don't really know with a renewed sense of curiosity so you can help your student find what she's always had inside but perhaps never noticed. Help her see possibilities with a positive attitude.*

- *Focus on* dialogue, *not* feedback.

Give your student the chance to examine her thoughts and actions and make decisions based on deeper understanding.

- *Suspend your own judgments, prejudices, and assumptions so you'll be fully present with your student each time you get together to discuss career-related issues.*

Encourage Reflection

Reflection deepens learning. So it's critical for your student to spend time reflecting upon his thoughts and feelings after he makes key career decisions and takes action on them.

You can help by asking open-ended questions: "How did it feel to _____ ?" or "How does this experience impact your choices so far?" You might even want to encourage your student to keep a journal where he can examine such questions and write out his responses to them in depth.

Preparing to Use the Parent Guide

As you go through the process of career coaching your college student using this *Parent Guide*, your goal will be to listen, question, and encourage in a way that will help your student develop a solid plan of action—and the confidence to then carry out that plan. You should seek not necessarily to reach *decisions* (those will come in time), but rather to get your student moving so she can "reality test" her career dreams.

Helping your student discover and uncover what she already knows in some conscious or unconscious way is precisely what career coaches do. You're *assisting* your student; you're not *deciding for* her. Only she can write her own unique career story. Your job is to empower her to feel comfortable with you throughout the career development process, and to go beyond her comfort zone when necessary to realize her own internal dreams—with your full support. It's one of the most critical tasks you'll ever undertake. It's also one of the most rewarding.

Let's begin.

A Word About Gender Usage

Throughout this *Parent Guide*, we alternate between using masculine and feminine pronouns—*he* and *she*, *him* and *her*, and so on—so that we can be inclusive in our wording but avoid awkward and sometimes confusing sentence constructions featuring *he/she*, *him/her*, and the like.

Freshman Year

Exploration

Introduction

Your student has finally made it to campus! This is an exciting time of his life. It's his first opportunity to really explore the career and academic possibilities that are unfolding in front of him.

Your student has a lot of choices to make during this first year of school—in fact, during his first few *weeks* of school. These decisions will set the course for his first semester and, indeed, his entire first-year experience.

Paying attention to academics is your student's top priority at this point. The experiences he carries from high school may or may not be in line with what his college/university is expecting of him now. So his best bet is to take charge of his course work from the beginning. Maybe your student hasn't ever mastered studying. If that's the case, encourage him—strongly if necessary—to brush up on his skills and ask for help (which, by the way, is almost always available right on campus). The college/university wants your student to succeed. So encourage him to take advantage of the many resources the campus has to offer.

Your student should take a wide variety of courses this year so that he can explore his interests and identify possible majors. As the year goes along, encourage your student to work hard to earn good grades, to get to know his academic advisor and at least one of his professors, and to start thinking about how his first year of college will tie into his future career—because it will.

Parent/Student Road Map Activities

How Deeply Does Your Student Know Herself?

How can your college student begin to capture and understand her essence and study it for its relevance to her life decisions? Encourage your student to give careful thought to the questions that follow and write down her responses in detail.

• PARENT TIP •

It's a good idea to do your own self-assessment before you begin these exercises with your student. So take a few minutes to think carefully about how well (or poorly!) you knew yourself when you were your student's age. Do you remember what you thought of yourself? How you defined success? What brought you joy? Write down your recollections.

Next, ask yourself a different question: What do you want to do when you're finished with your own career?

Retire? Volunteer? What do you want to accomplish in the next several years? What has made you really satisfied with your career? Answering these questions will put you in the same psychological "place" as your student (albeit in a different stage of life), which will give you a firsthand idea of how this career development process feels.

Share your thoughts with your student before you begin this exercise so that she doesn't feel pressure to immediately come up with perfect answers for each question. Indeed, assure your student that she'll most likely be unable to answer each question with perfect clarity and finality.

By participating fully in this activity as a parent, you model the depth with which your student needs to think about the questions that make up the activity.

Part One

Answer these questions yourself and encourage your student to do the same so that you can share your insights with each other when you're done:

What brings you joy?

_____

_____

What do you daydream about when you're alone?

_____

_____

What do you enjoy reading?

_____

_____

What is the one thing in your life that, if taken away, would leave you feeling completely lost and unhappy?

_____

_____

How do you currently define your personal identity? (That is, how do you derive meaning from your daily life? What are the various ways you identify yourself—e.g., student, avid reader, lifelong learner, athlete, future advertising professional)?

_____

_____

_____

How do you (or how would you like to) define your professional identity? Who are you at this moment in life?

_____

_____

How do you feel about yourself, and how do you want to feel about yourself in a career?

_____

_____

What are your "triggers"—the "buttons" that, when pushed, bring on anxiety and stress? How do you deal with these triggers/buttons in a healthy way?

_____

_____

How do you want others to see you?

_____

_____

_____

What feelings do you want to get from your job to make it worth doing each day for a significant period of time?

_____

_____

_____

_____

What do you really want out of life?

_____

_____

_____

What are your *innate talents*—the abilities that come easily and naturally to you?

_____

_____

_____

_____

What draws out the best in you? When are you motivated to do well? Why?

_____

_____

_____

_____

_____

• P A R E N T   T I P •

In the past several months, what have you shared with your student about your career? How has this information influenced her? Does she see work as a part of life in a balanced way?

Reflect upon how your conversations and comments might influence your student. Then decide if there's anything you need to do to make sure she begins to develop her own sense of what work is to her.

Part Two

Think back to when your student was very young. Read the following questions and share what you remember about your student from when she was an infant through her early teen years:

What did your student spend a significant portion of time doing as a child? (Examples: created beautiful art, sang to herself, made model airplanes, completed puzzles, went outside looking for bugs.)

_____

_____

_____

_____

_____

_____

What did your student do well from the time she was little?
(Examples: played nicely with others, played well alone, played a
musical instrument competently, did well in spelling, asked good
questions, showed a good work ethic.)

_____

_____

_____

_____

_____

What did your student receive the most compliments on when she was
little? (Examples: detailed and timely with her homework, showed
kindness to others, took initiative.)

_____

_____

_____

_____

What do you remember that created stress or anxiety for your student
when she was little? (Examples: taking tests, being left with a sitter,
attending large-group events.)

_____

_____

_____

_____

_____

Part Three

Share with your student your responses to the preceding questions. Then discuss the following questions with her:

What patterns do you see in the responses? Any light bulbs coming on for either of you?

Do you see any clues about the innate talents your student has?

Do you see any clues about your student's interests?

Do you see any clues in your student's previous behaviors?

Does your student see meaning in any of these recollections?

Uncover Your Student's Hidden Passions

Passion is a very individual concept, and it involves connecting your head with your heart. Passion bubbles up from our core. It's internal. So it's often a challenging subject for college students—especially since academia tends to be very cerebral and in many ways an external experience. Quite often, college students—particularly freshmen—learn by acting merely as receivers of information (through lectures and the like) rather than truly examining new information against what they know to be true from their own experience and knowledge.

Identifying passions is difficult for practically everybody—but especially for someone like your college student who is trying to find a future career path. The key to unlocking your student's potential career passions is *exposing her to a wide range of options*. Here are a few things you and your student can do to get started on the passion identification process:

• PARENT TIP •

*Pay close attention to your student's excitement.
What's behind that excitement?
Pay attention to your own excitement as well. What's behind your excitement? Your answers to these questions suggest where your passions lie. (An important note: We all have our own very personal experience with our passions.
So be careful not to judge your student's passions or dissuade her from following those passions.
It's an easy trap to fall into, unfortunately, because you don't know what's going on inside your student's head and heart.
So listen carefully, without judgment, and you'll hear what your student's passions truly are.)*

1. Make a list of any inspirations you've had that you haven't yet acted upon, and have your student do the same thing. Discuss your respective ideas with each other. Next, each of you should choose one idea that is most meaningful to you. Together, create action steps that will help you bring each inspiration closer to reality.

2. Consider the following discussion questions as you work through this activity:

- What were you doing the last time you lost all track of time?
- What might this knowledge reveal about your future career aspirations?

3. If you'd like, you and your student can each pick another idea from your original lists and repeat this activity.

Where Interests and
Abilities Align, There Lies Career Possibility

It's important for your student to understand how to identify and sort through his innate talents (abilities), skills, and interests. Doing so will help him home in on key clues that will in turn allow him to weed through his many career options.

• PARENT TIP •

Your student may have a difficult time identifying his innate talents (abilities), skills, and interests. You can help by asking him about the various activities he's involved in and helping him name the skills he uses in these activities (e.g., interpersonal skills, communication skills, computer skills, problem-solving skills, physical skills like balance and stamina).

The goal is to help your student identify careers that speak to his innate talents, his skills, and his interests and passions. So encourage your student to do the following:

1. *Make a list of your top fifteen abilities and skills (e.g., strong research skills, good interpersonal abilities, sound listening skills, well-above-average writing abilities).*

2. *Make a list of your top fifteen interests (e.g., favorite academic subjects, favorite activities, favorite places, favorite things to talk about).*

3. *Look for items that appear on both of these lists—i.e., areas where your abilities/skills and interests line up. What do you notice about these items?*

What careers could your student explore that might tap what he is both good at and passionate about? Encourage your student to look into these careers. One good way to start is to simply read about them. The U.S. Department of Labor's online Occupational Outlook Handbook is a great place to begin (www.bls.gov/oco). Most bookstores and libraries also carry a wide variety of career exploration resources.

Decision Making Is a Learned Skill

Want to find out how your student makes decisions? Then do the following exercise together:

1. Write down two or three decisions you've made in the last few weeks.

   _____

   _____

   _____

2. Answer the following questions about those decisions:

   What was the first thing you did to get started on the decision-making process?

   _____

   _____

   What did you do next? and next?

   _____

   _____

   _____

How did you finally make your decision?

_____

_____

_____

_____

_____

_____

_____

_____

_____

_____

_____

_____

Example: *I wanted to learn how to play the guitar. I researched the types of guitars, then went to a few guitar stores and had the clerks play different brands so I could hear how each one sounded. Then I spoke with a guy at one of the stores about renting a guitar and taking lessons. I asked a few friends who play guitar about their experiences learning guitar and about different types of guitars. I borrowed a guitar from a friend for a few weeks to make decisions about buying or renting. I then borrowed a different guitar and figured out it was the type of guitar I wanted. I then had to decide whether I wanted to own a guitar before I learned how to play or to rent one instead. I decided to sign up for a rent-to-own agreement and chose a used guitar. I signed up for lessons through the local community education program, which was inexpensive.*

3. Examine the methods you used in making this decision:

Did you analyze data and engage in research?

_____

_____

Did you discuss the decision with other people?

_____

_____

Did you just "know" or have an intuitive/gut feeling?

_____

_____

Was it an emotional decision—e.g., the guitar was so beautiful you just had to have it?

_____

_____

Was your decision simply a reaction?

_____

_____

Were there outside influencers (e.g., parents, other adults)? Were there any mind influencers (i.e., the "shoulds")?

_____

_____

4. Write down the process you went through to make your decision.

_____

_____

_____

_____

_____

_____

_____

_____

_____

5. How well did your decision-making process work? Was the outcome what you wanted? How could you improve your decision-
   making process?

_____

_____

_____

_____

_____

_____

_____

_____

Once you've both completed this exercise, discuss what you've discovered.

Sharing with your student how you make decisions will show her that we're all different when it comes to decision making. It will also teach her the strengths of your style and illuminate when and where you might be a good resource for her when she's making decisions of her own.

Academic Activities

Orientation

Encourage your student to attend orientation and register for classes— and be sure you attend the school's parent orientation if one is offered.

Why

Academic success actually starts before your student officially arrives on campus. *Orientation* will be his foundation, for many reasons. He'll be given excellent academic information, he'll register for his first classes, he'll learn about campus resources, and he'll start to connect with people. He may even make his first friends. The school knows what your student and his fellow freshmen need to understand before they arrive on campus, so make sure your student attends orientation.

How

1. Your student will have already received many mailings from the admissions and orientation departments of his school. He'll need to register for a particular orientation program in advance. Most schools expect students to attend a two-day program and will often invite you to attend as well. If your student hasn't taken math and foreign language placement tests prior to attending orientation, he can expect to take them prior to registering for his first classes.

2. Your student should attend orientation on the date he has registered for—more than likely sometime in June or July. Encourage him not to put off attending orientation until just prior to classes starting; if he does, he'll likely be behind from the beginning.

• ROAD MAP QUESTIONS TO ASK YOUR STUDENT •

Passions: Are you passionate about attending the school you've chosen? Did orientation get you excited for your upcoming first semester?

Innate talents: During orientation, did you meet with an academic advisor that you can see yourself talking to for the next year to explore your academic and career interests and strengths?

What matters most: Will this school be a place where you feel at home? Do you feel like you connected with a few people—students, faculty, staff—during orientation? Can you build solid relationships with some of these people over the next year or so?

Core Courses

Encourage your student to use her required general education *core courses* to take a wide variety of classes, even in disciplines she's not familiar with.

Why

Most schools require students to take a certain number of *core courses*. These courses ensure (from the institution's perspective) that every student who graduates from the school has been generally exposed to a wide range of ideas—in the arts, the sciences, social issues, communication (written and oral), and other essential areas.

If your student plays her cards right, she can use the core course requirements to explore disciplines and the careers associated with those disciplines—because if your student is like most college students (especially freshmen), she's aware of only a *tiny* fraction of the careers that exist in the world of work. (Did you know that there are more than twenty thousand specific job titles out there, with the number growing every day?)

Remember: Your student wasn't born passionate about whatever it is she's passionate about right now. Whether it's sports, music, writing, or something else, at some point she didn't *know* she enjoyed that activity so much; she had to expose herself to it (or *be exposed* to it by someone or something else) before she was able to realize she liked it!

Inspire your student to use this same experimental attitude in choosing her core courses. She may discover a passion she didn't even know she had—which may potentially become an integral part of her future career.

How

1. Remind your student to set up a meeting with her assigned academic advisor shortly before she registers for classes for the upcoming semester. (She can set up this meeting via email, through a phone call, or by simply stopping by her advisor's office on campus.) Your student will want to discuss her course schedule for the upcoming semester—and, in particular, she will want to figure out how to take some classes that will let her explore careers/disciplines and meet her *core course* requirements at the same time.

2. Before your student meets with her advisor, she should look at the schedule of courses for the upcoming semester. Encourage her to talk with her friends and classmates about some of the classes *they* have taken. What did they like about their classes, and what did they learn? Maybe one of these courses would intrigue your student too.

3. When your student meets with her advisor, she should immediately reiterate one of her key goals: to take courses in a wide variety of disciplines while meeting her core course requirements at the same time.

4. Encourage your student to be open to courses her advisor suggests. After all, that advisor probably knows the institution better than your student does at this point. Encourage your student to tap that expertise.

5. It's OK if your student leaves her advising meeting *not* having decided on anything definite (yet). Give her a day or two to think about what she discussed with her advisor, and to do a little more research on certain courses she talked about.

6. Encourage your student to come up with two or three versions of her course schedule for the upcoming semester, all of which meet her goal of diversifying the courses she takes. As a freshman, your student may not get her first-choice courses and/or schedule each semester. So work with her to have a Plan B and a Plan C that are equally acceptable—before she goes to actually register.

7. Once your student is set with her courses, don't be alarmed if she has an immediately *negative* reaction to at least one of them once classes begin. After all, she may be exposing herself to a brand new topic, and so she may be intimidated by or bored with it. Encourage your student to give the questionable course a chance instead of running out and immediately dropping it!

• ROAD MAP QUESTIONS TO ASK YOUR STUDENT •

Passions: What topics do you already enjoy studying? As importantly, what topics *might* you enjoy studying if you were to give them a chance?

Innate talents: In what academic areas do you already excel? And in which areas *might* you excel if you were to give them a try?

What matters most: Which subjects/disciplines matter most to you? Why? Which matter least? Why?

First-Year Experience Course

Encourage your student to take a *First-Year Experience* (FYE) course offered by his school. (Note: These programs go by a number of names, including *University 101, freshman seminar, living/learning communities, courses in common,* and *block courses.*)

Why

Many schools offer their own variation of a *First-Year Experience* course. Some programs, typically called *University 101*, introduce students to the campus and the resources available to them, and help them with the transition from high school to college. Other programs focus on academic experiences. Examples: *freshman seminar, courses in common,* and *block courses.*

Your student will also want to see if his school offers *living/learning communities*, which allow students who are interested in the same areas of study to take courses together and live in the same residence hall/area.

All of these courses are designed to help your student succeed academically as a freshman. Often, the courses are taught by tenured faculty members and give students a priceless experience they would not otherwise have. That's especially important when your student is attending a larger school, where he may well find an introductory course that is as large as his entire high school class was!

How

1. Your student may receive information about *First-Year Experience* courses prior to orientation. If he doesn't, encourage him to ask his assigned academic advisor (or another campus representative)—during orientation—about these types of opportunities. Your student will need to consider whether an FYE course fits with his academic plans, but usually there are options for most everyone.

2. Encourage your student to talk with other students he knows who participate(d) in a *First-Year Experience* program at his institution. What do these students have to say about the program? Most students don't regret being a part of something that was designed especially for them.

3. If your student misses out on *First-Year Experience* opportunities during the fall, see if the courses are offered again during the spring semester. If they are, encourage your student to sign up.

• ROAD MAP QUESTIONS TO ASK YOUR STUDENT •

Passions: Do any of your *First-Year Experience* courses appeal to your interests? What excites you about them? Do you enjoy working with other students?

Innate talents: Are your professors and/or fellow students giving you any feedback on what you're good at? Are you surprised with what people are saying about your talents? Do you agree with these observations? Why or why not?

What matters most: Does learning in a community setting resonate with you? Why or why not?

"How to Study" Courses

Encourage your student to enroll in a "how to study" course.

Why

Fairly or unfairly, grades are important to most of the employers your student will one day pursue. For starters, if your student's grades are good, most employers will conclude that she has mastered essential workplace-related skills, like how to organize and manage her time, how to do research and communicate well, and how to break down complex ideas into manageable bites of information that are easy to understand.

On a more immediately practical level, many employers make their decisions about which students/grads to interview for jobs (and internships) based on their cumulative grade-point average (GPA)—e.g., "We only interview students/grads who have a 3.25 GPA or above." Fair? Of course not. But it's reality.

As a result, getting off to a bad start, grade-wise, during freshman year can be very difficult for your student to overcome. Specifically, getting her overall GPA to 3.0 or above (the minimum many employers will consider) by the time junior and senior year roll around could prove daunting at best and impossible at worst.

How

1. Encourage your student to set up an appointment with the academic advisor who has been assigned to her—that is, the person who helps her choose which courses to take each semester. (Depending on the school, this person will either be a full-time academic advisor or a member of the general faculty.) Your student can email her advisor, call him/her, or simply stop by his/her office.) Your student should tell her advisor that she's interested in learning about any programs or short courses the school offers on "how to study."

2. If the school has its own academic advising center, your student should go there and ask one of the advisors if the center (or another department on campus) offers any programs or short courses on "how to study."

3. Once your student has identified the "how to study" programs that are available on campus, encourage her to sign up for one of them and

attend its meetings faithfully. Asking questions about things she doesn't understand and doing her best to implement (in her classes) the academic strategies she's learning will put her on the right track.

4. When the program ends, encourage your student to ask the instructor if it would be OK for her to contact him/her again in the future if she has other concerns. (Invariably, the instructor will say yes.)

5. After your student has been using some of her newfound academic strategies for, say, a semester, encourage her to set up an appointment with the person who taught the study program and ask for help with anything she's still struggling with when it comes to her academics. No one expects your student to master every new academic skill the first time.

• ROAD MAP QUESTIONS TO ASK YOUR STUDENT •

Passions: What academic *activities*—research, writing, reading, organizing—excite you the most? Which academic *subjects* excite you the most?

Innate talents: What study techniques come easily to you? Conversely, what areas do you need help with?

What matters most: Does doing well in school matter to you? What priority do you place on getting good grades?

Role of the Academic Advisor

Encourage your student to meet with his academic advisor at least twice each semester.

Why

At most schools, students are required to meet with their academic advisors only once each semester, and they *have* to go to that meeting to get the formal institutional approval they need to register for the next semester's courses. If your student sets up and attends *another* meeting with his academic advisor each semester, he can go beyond merely checking in and getting his advisor to sign off on his upcoming course schedule. Instead, your student can talk about how his courses are going, what he's enjoying and not enjoying, what's going well for him academically, and what's not going so well.

It's the "not enjoying" and "not going so well" activities that are of greatest concern here. Your student's advisor can use this second meeting with your student to point him toward resources, right on campus, that can help him address—and perhaps fix—whatever it is that he's struggling with from an academic standpoint. The results will be better grades, higher satisfaction, and, as importantly, a boost in your student's confidence— all traits that are sought by the employers he'll be trying to impress not so long from now.

How

1. Remind your student to set up a second meeting with his academic advisor—a half-hour session where he can talk about how his classes are going.

2. Before the meeting, your student should write up a brief list of the things he'd like to discuss with his advisor. Your student can think in terms of four broad areas:

   - Which courses he's doing well in, and why.
   - Which courses he's struggling with, and why.
   - Which courses he enjoys the most, and why.
   - Which courses he enjoys the least, and why.

3. Encourage your student to type up his list of questions and bring them to the meeting. He should bring a copy for his advisor as well so that the advisor can look at the questions during the session.

4. During this meeting with his advisor, your student should stress that he is not demanding any magic answers or startling revelations. Instead, he should simply say that he's taking stock of where he's at and that he's interested in any ideas his advisor has for him. Then he should just let the meeting run its course. Your student will never know what, if anything, is going to happen at a particular meeting. But it's almost impossible to leave an advising meeting worse off. (If this happens to your student, however, tell him not to be afraid to seek out a new advisor.)

5. After the meeting, your student should email his advisor a brief thank-you note for his/her time. Your student will stand out for this seemingly simple act alone, thus improving the relationship for the long term. He'll also get the chance to practice writing good thank-you notes—which will be essential when he's talking to employers about internships and jobs later in college.

• R O A D   M A P   Q U E S T I O N S   T O   A S K   Y O U R   S T U D E N T •

Passions: Did your advisor suggest any courses or strategies that (a) match your current interests, and/or (b) pique interests you didn't know you had?

Innate talents: Did your advisor suggest any courses or strategies that (a) match what you're already good at, and/or (b) reveal what you didn't *know* you were good at?

What matters most: What patterns are starting to develop in your conversations with your advisor? Are you talking about how your academic plan will give you the life you want to live—whatever that means to you?

Meeting with Professors
Encourage your student to use the office hours offered by her professors.

Why
Research has shown time and again that the better students connect with their professors at college, the more likely they'll be to stay *in* college and finish their degree. Attending office hours is the easiest way for your student to begin connecting with her professors.

Office hours give your student the chance to ask questions she may not feel comfortable bringing up in class. If your student is struggling in a certain course, the professor can help her with learning strategies for that particular subject.

Your student will be seeing her professors perhaps more than any other people on campus. It only makes sense, then, that the better your student gets to know her professors—and helps her professors get to know her—the greater the chance she'll be successful in college.

There's even more to the story. Later in her college career, when your student is looking for an internship or even that first job after graduation, she's going to need a few *references*—people who can speak highly of her and her work. If she invests time and energy now in developing a good relationship with at least one professor, she'll have someone who is both willing and able to tell prospective employers good things about her.

Think about it this way: Which student will be most impressive to a prospective employer—one who merely *says* she has, for instance, strong research skills, or one whose English professor has *seen* those strong research skills in action and can thus tell employers of their authenticity?

How

1. Encourage your student to attend office hours at least one time for each class she's in during the semester.

2. Your student will need to go into these meetings prepared to take the lead in the discussion with her professor. When the professor invariably asks, "So … what is it that you wanted to talk about?" your student must be ready to say something like this: "I'm just interested in the things we're talking about in class. I'd like to learn more about them. Do you have any suggestions about books I could read or web sites I could visit that would cover more of the basics?" Then, your student can see what her professor has to say.

3. If your student is struggling in class, encourage her to be ready to share this information with her professor and to ask for help.

4. Your student should take a few notes on her professor's suggestions and be ready to answer questions that might come up during the course of the discussion.

5. Remind your student to keep an eye on the clock and to take the initiative to wrap up the meeting when the allotted time has passed. She should also be sure to send a brief thank-you note to the professor a day or two after the meeting.

Passions: Did your professor tell you about any resources, courses, or even careers that sound interesting to you? that you've never heard of before?

Innate talents: Did your professor happen to point out to you that you're good at something related to the course—understanding the basic principles being discussed, for example, or developing and writing solid research papers?

What matters most: Are there specific topics you like discussing with an expert (i.e., your professor)? What are they? Why are they so compelling to you?

Investigating Potential Majors

Encourage your student to check out three to five majors that **seem** to have the potential for matching his passions, innate talents, and values—i.e., majors that are probably worth investigating in more depth. (No need to *choose* one yet, though! There's plenty of time for that later!)

Why

At most schools, students will have to decide on a *major* at some point—that is, the discipline to which they'll devote most of their academic time and energy. At most four-year institutions, students are required to declare a major once they've accumulated enough credits to be considered a junior—in other words, at or near the end of their sophomore year.

It's very easy to fall into the trap of thinking that if your student doesn't choose the "right" major the first time, he's doomed. That is simply false. In fact, statistics show that many college students change their declared major at least once before they graduate, and some students change their major more than once.

• FACT •

In the 2005 Graduating Student & Alumni Survey *conducted by the National Association of Colleges and Employers (a trade organization made up of college/university career services professionals and employers who hire new college graduates):*

- *More than 1 in 4 (26.5%) of the 750+ respondents said they had* changed their major once during their college years.

- *More than 1 in 10 (12.1%) said they had changed their major twice during their college years.*

- *Almost 1 in 10 (9%) said they had changed their major three or more times during their college years.*

Your student can save considerable time, energy, and perhaps even heartache later on by starting to fully explore majors *now*, during his freshman year. He can take the time to look around a bit, see what majors are out there and what they're about, and make an informed choice.

Think of it this way: If you were going to buy yourself a new outfit, wouldn't you be more likely to pick one you really like by starting early and studying as many options as you can—versus running into a store at the last minute and grabbing the first thing you see? The same logic applies when your student is choosing a major.

Choosing a major is a pretty critical decision, after all. As researchers from the Center for Labor Market Studies at Northeastern University have found (and written about in the *College Majors Handbook*—JIST Publishing, 2004), the typical employer is more interested in what your student has majored in at school versus what school he has attended.

While the major your student selects isn't the be-all-end-all that will define his entire career, it *is* one of the more important decisions he'll make during his college years.

How

1. Help your student find the online or printed version of his school's academic *catalog* (sometimes called the *bulletin* or *course guide*). On the school's web site, you'll usually find this information under a broad section entitled "Academics" or "Programs and Majors." Conversely, you can usually find the printed version of an institution's academic catalog at the admissions office or at a campus-wide academic advising center.

2. Your student should take an hour or two to read through *all* of his school's academic majors and programs. It's important for him to not rule out any major at this point—especially when it comes to his abilities (or perceived lack thereof). For each program or major, encourage your student to ask the following question: "My abilities aside, does this program/major sound *interesting* to me?"

3. Have your student highlight or write down each major that does sound interesting to him. (Remember: We're talking only about your student's *interests* at this point! For now, he shouldn't worry about whether he thinks he'd be any good at a particular major/program.)

4. Encourage your student to keep a separate list of majors he knows nothing about. If, for a particular major, your student's honest answer to the question posed in No. 2 above is "I have no idea—I don't even know what this major is!", he should write that major down on this second list. (Note: Wouldn't it be tragic if your student passed up on a potentially satisfying major because he said "no" to the question in No. 2 above when his response really should have been "I don't know"?)

• F A C T •

According to research by Northeastern University economists Paul Harrington, Neeta Fogg, and Thomas Harrington, it's one's college major—rather than the college or university one attends— that may just be the ticket into (or out of) a financially sound and rewarding professional life.

~ Northeastern University news release, August 5, 2004

5. Once your student has his two lists completed—one of majors that sound interesting to him, the other of majors he honestly knows nothing about—have him take the first list and, as best he can, prioritize which majors sound *most* interesting right now. Encourage your student to pick his "Top 5" as of now. These are the majors he'll use to *begin* his exploration.

6. From the second list, your student should pick two majors at random and commit to at least reading a bit about them, at a minimum.

7. Once your student has finished his two lists, encourage him to add to (or subtract from) them by:

   • Talking to friends who are near the end of their college career and who have already chosen a major. What do they like (or dislike) about their major? Why did they choose it?

   • Talking with friends of your family who already have careers that interest your student. What did these people major in during college? What did they like (or dislike) about those majors?

   • Talking with you about your own college major if you attended college.

8. Remind your student of this essential point: "Your goal right now is not to decide what major to *choose*; for now, the idea is to simply decide what majors to *explore first!*"

• ROAD MAP QUESTIONS TO ASK YOUR STUDENT •

Passions: What areas of interest have you always been drawn to? What did you dream about when you were little?

Innate talents: Have you been able to take classes to explore the things you're good at? Are you successful in these courses at the college level?

What matters most: Do you have a sense of your life's purpose at this point, or do you need to keep exploring the answer to this question?

Value of International Study

Encourage your student to explore the possibility of studying abroad for a semester during her sophomore or junior year of college.

Why

A study abroad experience opens your student's eyes to a different culture and forces her to adapt to that culture very quickly—a skill that will be admired by prospective employers in the future. Study abroad also teaches your student unique skills and introduces her to what is becoming an increasingly global world economy and job market.

> Study abroad does more than promote academic enrichment and personal growth. It also can enhance your employment prospects, especially in the fields of business, international affairs, and government service. Employers increasingly seek graduates who have studied abroad. They know that students who have successfully completed a study abroad program are likely to possess international knowledge and, often, second-language skills. Such students are also likely to have other transnational competencies that graduate and professional schools and employers value just as highly: cross-cultural communication skills, analytical skills, an understanding of and familiarity with local customs and cultural contexts, flexibility, resilience, and the ability to adapt to new circumstances and deal constructively with differences.
>
> *~ Institute of International Education web site*

How

1. Your student can check out the school's web site to find information about the institution's study abroad department or office.

2. Encourage your student to visit the study abroad office/department and to pick up general information on study abroad opportunities offered through the school.

3. Your student should ask if she can meet individually with an advisor in the study abroad office/department, or if there are any upcoming introductory sessions for students who are interested in potentially studying abroad.

4. Encourage your student to ask her academic advisor, her professors, a campus career counselor (at the school's career center), and her friends if they know anyone who is currently studying abroad or who has done so in the past. Your student should get the names of these students and contact them to see what studying abroad is really like.

5. Direct your student to the web sites of organizations like the Council on International Educational Exchange (www.ciee.org) and the Institute of International Education (www.iie.org) to learn more about study abroad possibilities.

• ROAD MAP QUESTIONS TO ASK YOUR STUDENT •

Passions: Have you ever dreamed about living in another country? Where? Do you know why?

Innate talents: Could you adapt to a new environment and a different culture? Would you be comfortable if you didn't speak the language? Can you communicate in other ways?

What matters most: Is it important, in your mind, to learn about the world beyond the borders of the United States? Why or why not?

Experiential Activities

Living on Campus

Encourage your student to live on campus if at all possible.

Why

Living on campus will help your student become comfortable with his new surroundings and make friends. He'll also be able to more easily attend programs directed toward his interests and uncover ways to get involved—and involvement is the key to success at college.

Be prepared to guide your student through roommate struggles and adjusting to life in a small space. But the memories of living on campus last a lifetime for your student. Indeed, he will most likely meet his college friends—the ones he'll hang out with for the next few years (and, in some cases, beyond)—during his first weeks living on campus.

Remember, too, that one of the key traits future employers will be looking for is your student's ability to get along with other people. (On your student's second-grade report card, this trait was probably evaluated in a section called "works and plays well with others"!) By living on campus, your student will quickly meet people who come from all walks of life and who have widely differing views of the world.

How

1. Help your student fill out an on-campus housing application. Make sure he turns it in promptly along with any associated application fees. Living on campus is competitive at many schools when it comes to the particular residence hall your student might want or the type of room he desires.

2. Prepare your student to meet his roommate. The school's housing office will send him the name of his roommate sometime during the summer. Encourage your student to contact his roommate prior to move-in day so that he can get to know this other student a bit—and determine who's bringing what in terms of living possessions.

3. Help your student keep an open mind regarding his future roommate. Let him know that it isn't necessary to be best friends with his roommate, but that he'll have a much better year if he finds ways to get along with this new person. (At the same time, he'll learn the key negotiating and problem-solving skills he'll eventually need in, say, an internship setting or his first-job workplace.)

• ROAD MAP QUESTIONS TO ASK YOUR STUDENT •

Passions: What are you learning about yourself by living on campus, and perhaps with someone new?

Innate talents: What compliments are you receiving from your new college friends? Do they seem to be spotting in you skills and abilities you didn't even know you had?

What matters most: What kind of people are you spending time with—especially if you're in your first few weeks of college? How are they influencing you and your decision making? Are you happy with how things are going so far? Are you being yourself, or are you trying to be someone you're not?

"Welcome Week" Activities

Encourage your student to get involved at her new school by attending "Welcome Week" and convocation activities.

Why

Believe it or not, your student's school has been planning for her arrival for more than a year. The people at the school have thought about how they can make each student feel like part of the campus community, and they've planned a variety of "Welcome Week" activities for all new freshmen. Indeed, events like convocation and other ceremonial activities are initiations into the academic traditions of the school. Your student won't want to miss the experience of being with her classmates as they are all formally welcomed to the institution.

The residence hall, the student union, student clubs, fraternities and sororities, and other campus organizations will have activities offering the opportunity for students to get involved. Talk to your student about what she'd like to participate in during her first semester on campus. Encourage your student to pick something that is interesting to her, and that will teach her something helpful for her future career.

How

1. The school will give out information about student activities fairs, convocation, and similar events starting at orientation. Your student should watch for this information and attend the events that will motivate her and get her involved.

2. Encourage your student to grab a few of her new friends and get out of the residence hall during the first few days of school. Challenge your student to explore a bit.

3. Your student can get advice about activities from her residence hall's *resident assistant* (RA) or *community advisor* (CA). This veteran student

will have great tips about what activities are worth your student's time and energy.

Passions: What special events did you attend during the opening days of school, and how did they make you feel? Are you excited about involving yourself in a particular organization that interests you? Are you going to join? Why or why not?

Innate talents: Throughout all of the activities you've participated in, what felt easiest to you? Did you feel comfortable going alone? Did you prefer to bring a friend?

What matters most: Do you feel more connected now that you've found some options for campus involvement? Do you feel your school is a good fit for you? Why or why not?

Campus Organizations
Encourage your student to join at least one campus organization.

Why
Year after year, when employers across the United States are surveyed about the key *soft skills* they look for as they consider college students for internships and jobs, they consistently give the highest rankings to strong communication skills, the ability to work well with other people in small groups or teams, demonstrated self-motivation and initiative, and proven leadership skills.

In the *Job Outlook 2005* survey—conducted by the National Association of Colleges and Employers (a trade association for college/university career services professionals and employers who hire new college graduates)—employers were asked to rank the importance of a variety of soft skills in new college graduates (with 5 being "extremely important" and 1 being "not important"). The top-rated skills (and their average scores):

Communication skills (written and verbal) 4.7

Honesty/integrity 4.7

Interpersonal skills (relates well with others) 4.5

Strong work ethic 4.5

Teamwork skills (works well with others) 4.5

Analytical skills 4.4

Motivation/initiative 4.4

Flexibility/adaptability 4.3

Computer skills 4.2

Detail orientation 4.1

Leadership skills 4.0

Organizational skills 4.0

What better way for your student to show he has some or all of these key characteristics than to join and eventually get heavily involved in a campus organization? Encourage your student to think about focusing on a group that is geared to a discipline or field that interests him, or one that fits a special interest of his (e.g., the ski club or residence hall government).

Employers aren't naive—they know the difference between the student who joined a campus organization last semester of *senior* year in an attempt to build his resumé and the student who joined a campus group *freshman* year and became an integral part of its ongoing success. One is a pretender; the other is the real deal.

How

1. Encourage your student to ask a few of his classmates about what student groups they're aware of and, especially, how he can find out about *all* of the existing student groups on campus.

2. If your student is taking a class that covers topics of great interest, encourage him to ask the professor about campus organizations on campus that relate to the topic in question.

3. Tell your student to visit the web sites of the school's Student Activities and/or Student Organizations office. (Alternatively, your student can look for a mention of this office in the school's printed student handbook.) Someone on campus has a list of *all* campus organizations at the school.

4. If your student's school offers a "Campus Involvement Fair" or a "Student Activities Fair" (typically at the beginning of the school year),

make sure he considers attending. At this event, various campus organizations set up displays so they can recruit new members.

5. Once your student has identified a few campus groups that sound interesting, encourage him to contact a student leader of each group to learn more.

6. Encourage your student to attend meetings of the organizations that interest him most. Which groups seem to be thriving? Which ones aren't doing so well? Can your student see himself fitting in with one of these groups and perhaps even becoming a leader of that group someday?

7. Your student should pick one group and become a consistent meeting attendee. If an opportunity comes along for your student to volunteer in some small way, encourage him to take advantage of it. Your student should *not*, however, take on so much that he ends up feeling overwhelmed. One or two quality experiences are much better than four or five unsatisfying, surface-level experiences.

• ROAD MAP QUESTIONS TO ASK YOUR STUDENT •

Passions: What activities do you like (or might you like if you tried them)? Why?

Innate talents: What are you good at doing, especially in a group setting? What skills—especially *soft skills* (e.g., teamwork, communicating effectively)—are you obtaining or could you obtain in the campus organizations you're considering?

What matters most: What matters to you when it comes to how you spend your limited free time as well as your limited energy? Why?

Volunteer Activities
Encourage your student to devote a little time and energy to volunteer activities.

Why
Volunteering is a great way for your student to learn about different career possibilities and settings, build skills, and demonstrate her ability to man-

age her time and energy well. Moreover, volunteers are sorely needed in cities large and small across the entire United States.

There's another way your student will benefit from volunteering: Most prospective employers have profound respect for students who have done volunteer work. Why? Because volunteering shows employers that your student cares about people and issues beyond those in her own daily life. It demonstrates that she's willing to help address problems—if only in a small way—instead of merely complaining about them.

Your student will also discover that many employers are involved in volunteer activities themselves, so your student might well meet her future internship supervisor or employer while, for example, she's helping to build a Habitat for Humanity house or developing the web site for a local nonprofit agency.

How

1. Many colleges and universities have a Service-Learning office or Volunteer Center (or similarly named office) that serves as a clearinghouse for volunteer opportunities in the local area. If your student's school has such a center, encourage her to stop by that office sometime soon to see if there are any volunteer activities she could pursue. Even if your student is able to devote only an hour or two a month to volunteering, it will make a difference—to her and to the people and organizations that need the help.

2. If your student's school doesn't have a Service-Learning office or Volunteer Center, encourage your student to visit the Student Activities office or Student Organizations office (or similarly named office) to see if it publicizes local volunteer opportunities.

3. In many larger cities, the United Way serves as the clearinghouse for most of the volunteer activities in the area. If your student lives in a decent-sized city, she should contact the local United Way to see if it can help her uncover volunteer opportunities. (Visit the United Way web site at www.unitedway.org.) Your student can also use the VolunteerMatch web site (www.volunteermatch.org) to search for volunteer opportunities in a given geographic area.

4. Tell your student to check the local newspaper to see if it has a section called "Volunteers Needed" or something similar. (Many newspapers offer this service, for free, to help local organizations recruit volunteers.)

• ROAD MAP QUESTIONS TO ASK YOUR STUDENT •

Passions: Is the volunteer activity you're involved in something you might like to do for a living someday? Why or why not?

Innate talents: Are you good at the activity(ies) you're performing as a volunteer? Or could you be if you were to gain some more experience?

What matters most: Does the cause behind each of your volunteer activities matter to you—so much so that you might want to make a career out of it someday? Why or why not?

Part-Time Work

If your student has been successful academically, encourage him to find a part-time job, either on campus or off. (If your student has been struggling academically, he'll need to evaluate whether he can add this activity to his plate right now.)

Why

The college students of yesteryear could often get by without picking up any job experience during college. Back then, a college degree was typically seen as enough—on its own—for a student or recent graduate to land an entry-level job. Those days are gone—long gone. If you and your student don't believe it, listen to the employers who are surveyed each year by the National Association of Colleges and Employers (a trade association for college/university career services professionals and employers who hire new college graduates). In NACE's *Job Outlook 2005* survey, employers were asked to rank the importance of various types of work experience in new college graduates (with 5 being "extremely important" and 1 being "not important"). The top-rated experiences (and their average scores):

Relevant work experience 4.0
Internship experience 4.0
Any work experience 3.5
Co-op experience 3.4

The *College Hiring 2005* survey of employers—conducted by online job site CareerBuilder.com—underscores the point. When the more than six hundred participating employers were asked about the top characteristics they look for when hiring new college graduates for full-time, permanent jobs, the No. 1 answer (cited by 28 percent of the respondents) was "relevant experience." (Coming in at a distant No. 2—cited by just 12 percent of the respondents—was "professionalism during the interview.")

If you and your student can step into an employer's shoes for a moment, you'll begin to understand why experience is so critical to employers when they're evaluating college students and recent grads for jobs and internships. Bad hires cost a company thousands (or even millions, in the case of a large organization) of dollars a year. They also hurt company morale by frustrating the many *good* employees who are forced to work with less-than-ideal colleagues. By picking up some hands-on work experience during college—starting freshman year (if not before)—your student will show prospective employers that, first and foremost, he is able to *handle* basic (and often assumed … foolishly!) job tasks like showing up, being responsible, and working well with other people. Perhaps more importantly, your student will develop new skills, get a better sense of what he likes (and doesn't like!) about various work settings, and gather the evidence he'll need to *prove* to future employers that he can do what he's claiming he can do.

Of course, a little extra money in your student's pocket doesn't hurt either!

How

1. Your student can begin his part-time job search by looking in the classified section of the school's student newspaper. Many times, the companies that advertise jobs in college newspapers are looking specifically for college students who have flexible schedules.

2. Your student should also visit his school's career center to see if it offers—in print or, much more likely these days, online—a list of available part-time jobs in the city/area.

3. Many schools have a Student Employment Center (or similarly named office)—separate from the career center—whose sole purpose is helping students find part-time jobs. Does your student's school have such a resource? If so, encourage your student to tap it!

4. Your student should also scour the classified ads of the local off-campus newspaper (either in print or online). If your student lives in a large, urban area, he can scan not only the daily newspaper classifieds but also the classifieds of the many suburban papers in the area. (Note: Practically all newspapers these days make their classified ads available in print and online. So there's no need for your student to go out and actually track down physical copies of the many suburban newspapers in the area.)

5. Encourage your student to see if his city has a government-sponsored *workforce center* (or similarly named office). If it does, he can check out its web site for more part-time job listings.

6. Your student should ask some of his classmates about part-time jobs they're aware of. Are any of his friends or acquaintances working at places where they could help *him* get an interview for a job?

7. Ask your student, "Do any of your professors know about part-time jobs in the area that might serve the dual purpose of helping you get some experience in a field that truly interests you?" Your student's professors may have referred other students to these same organizations. Perhaps your student will be the next success story!

8. If campus resources leave your student dry, tell him to register with local staffing firms or temporary employment (*temp*) agencies to see what they have to offer. Temping is a great way for your student to gain exposure to various industries and make a little money. Plus, these organizations generally love working with college students, whose schedules are typically more flexible than most.

• ROAD MAP QUESTIONS TO ASK YOUR STUDENT •

Passions: Might you want to work in the field/setting/industry where you've landed a part-time job? Or have you instead discovered that this is *not* the field/industry/setting for you?

Innate talents: What do you do well in the part-time job you've landed? What specific skills are you gaining from it?

What matters most: Do the activities in your part-time job matter much to you, or are they merely "all in a day's work" as far as you're concerned?

The Career Portfolio

Encourage your student to start collecting items for the *career portfolio* she'll be building later on in her college career—the formal, three-ring binder that will feature, for instance, excellent papers she's written, brochures she's designed, awards she's won, research she's completed, and the like.

Why

Most employers have been burned a few times by people who have said (in an interview, for example) that they could or would do something but ultimately were unable to back up their words when they were on the job. The less-than-flattering term employers use for these people: "bad hires."

Employers, as one might imagine, don't want to make any bad hires. And so over time, they tend to become increasingly skeptical of the things they're told by job and internship seekers. They end up with an attitude that might be summarized—quite understandably—as "show me the proof!"

A *career portfolio* will give your student the proof she needs to back up her resumé and interview claims. Instead of merely *saying* to an employer, "I have strong communication skills" (to which an employer might mentally respond, "If I had a dime for every time I've heard that one …!"), your student will be able to *prove* she has strong communication skills by displaying the fifteen-page research paper on which her instructor wrote, "One of the best-written papers I've read in some time. Outstanding job!"

Eventually, your student's career portfolio will emerge in the form of a nice three-ring binder. (Think of it as a scrapbook with a career emphasis!) For now, though, all your student needs to do is start *keeping* and *collecting* the materials that might one day appear in her portfolio.

How

1. Your student will need to go to an office supply store and buy a large, plastic box with a cover. (It will cost under $10.)

2. Remind your student that whenever she creates or accomplishes something that carries even the slightest hint of her abilities and/or interests, she should put some result of that creation or accomplishment into her "career portfolio box." Example: Your student writes a simple computer program for a basic programming course. Encourage her to print out the code and put it in her career portfolio box. Another example: Your student's picture appears in the student newspaper during Campus Cleanup Day in the spring. She should cut out that picture, put it in a folder or some other protective covering, and save it in her career portfolio box.

3. If your student is ever in doubt about whether to bother keeping something or not, she should keep it! It's far better to save too many materials than too few. And what might seem irrelevant or unimportant today could turn out to be quite crucial tomorrow. Save, save, save!

4. If your student has the time and inclination, encourage her to visit her school's career center to see if someone there can either show her an example of a completed career portfolio or refer her to books that describe the concept in detail (with examples).

• ROAD MAP QUESTIONS TO ASK YOUR STUDENT •

Passions: As you look through the materials you're collecting in your career portfolio box, do you see any patterns when it comes to what you enjoy doing? Were any of the experiences associated with the materials especially enjoyable for you? Why?

Innate talents: What do the materials you're collecting demonstrate about your skills and abilities? If you want to prove to a future employer that you have, for example, solid teamwork skills, do you have any portfolio evidence to back up that claim? If not, how can you get some?

What matters most: What have you noticed in your collection of items that seems to be a recurring values-related theme? Do you see any clues about what will be important to you in your future career?

The Student Resumé

Encourage your student to write a first (and very rough!) draft of his resumé—knowing it will change considerably in the months and years to come.

Why

For better or worse, fairly or unfairly, prospective employers (for jobs and internships) will make their first judgments about your student by reading (or ... gasp ... tossing!) his resumé. So it's got to be good. If it isn't, the employer will choose someone else to interview and, ultimately, hire.

Fortunately, your student's resumé doesn't have to be good *immediately*—i.e., right now, during his freshman year. In fact, yours will be the rare student indeed—freshman or not—if he puts together an outstanding resumé on his first (or second or even third) attempt.

But none of that matters right now. All that matters is that your student gets something—anything—on paper. He can edit his resumé later, with the help of a career counselor at the school's career center, one or more of his favorite professors, or you. For now, your student just has to start. So encourage him to put some material to paper/screen, even if it's awful to begin with!

How

1. If he wants to, your student should try to write a draft resumé completely on his own at first. He can consult one of the dozens of resumé books on the market for ideas, or look for examples on the Internet.

2. Alternatively, your student could work on his resumé with the help of a career counselor at the school's career center. In reality, there is *no* need for your student to take on this important project all alone—especially when expert help is readily available at the campus career center. So if your student prefers the collaborative approach to writing a first-draft resumé, encourage him to go that route.

3. Your student may not need to actually use his resumé until months down the road—which is nice, as he'll have plenty of time to revise it. If, however, he needs a well-done resumé sooner versus later—to apply for a part-time job or an internship, for example—he'll need to take his

completed first draft to a campus career counselor or another knowledgeable person (e.g., a professor, a family friend, you) and ask for help
on improving it. Don't be surprised if it takes several revisions for your
student to get his resumé just so; no one writes a perfect resumé in only
one or two attempts!

4. As your student writes the various subsections of his resumé, he should
try to focus not simply on *duties* or generic *activities* from his past (e.g.,
"made calls") but instead on *accomplishments* and *achievements* (e.g.,
"helped raise $1,200 for Habitat for Humanity via cold calling"). His
career counselor can teach him more about this important distinction.

5. If your student is completely befuddled by this task, encourage him to
visit his school's career center for one-on-one resumé development
assistance.

• ROAD MAP QUESTIONS TO ASK YOUR STUDENT •

Passions: Does your first-draft resumé do a good job of showing
the reader what some of your key interests are? If not, how can you
improve it?

Innate talents: Does your first-draft resumé do an effective job of
documenting—as completely as possible—the skills and abilities you've
gained or used in your courses, student activities, jobs, and volunteer
work? Does it help the eventual reader understand what you've *done* and
what you *can do*?

What matters most: Have you highlighted accomplishments that are
truly important to you, such as community service, volunteering, or
other unique experiences that help define who you are?

The Campus Career Center

Encourage your student to visit the campus career center, and discuss with her what she learns about the available resources there.

Why

Practically every college/university in the United States has a career center. Whose money pays the bills for these career centers? Yours (and your student's, of course)—in the form of tuition and student fee dollars. (Note: Typically, the campus career center's services are free to students. But just remember that these "free" services are the result, in part, of the not-so-free tuition and fees you pay each semester!)

Of course, the money you and your student have invested is only part of the story (and a small one at that). Here are a few more practical reasons for your student to tap the resources of her school's career center—starting freshman year:

- It offers print, online, and people resources that will help her more easily explore majors and careers.

- It has statistics on the types of jobs obtained by past students from her school in various majors—so that she can easily learn, for example, what types of jobs have been landed by sociology majors ... or chemistry majors ... or _____ majors from her institution.

- It's staffed by professionals whose essential purpose is to help your student and others with complex career-related issues—through one-on-one counseling, courses, seminars, and computerized career guidance programs.

- It's where your student will eventually learn more about internship and co-op opportunities, perhaps interview for a post-graduation job, and do research on future educational endeavors like graduate or professional school.

How

1. Encourage your student to find the career center's link on the campus web site. (Note: At your student's school, the career center might be called the Office of Career Services or the Career Development Center or the Career Management Center or something else with the term

"career" in it.) Your student should click through to the career center's home page so she can see where the facility is located and how to contact someone there.

2. Depending on your student's personal preference, she can call or email the career center—or simply stop by—and tell the person who responds that she's a freshman and she'd like to learn about the resources available through the career center.

3. Your student may be asked if she'd like to see a particular counselor. If she honestly has no preference, she should go ahead and make an appointment with the person who is available the soonest. If your student *does* have a preference—someone who was very helpful to one of her friends, for example—encourage her to ask for that person by name, even if she has to wait a little longer to see that person. (Note: As is the case in any other business, some of the people who work at the career center will be more helpful than others. If your student can pick a helpful counselor the first time, so much the better!)

4. Your student should go to her first meeting ready to start working on one goal: learning about available resources. It's perfectly all right for your student to simply say to her counselor, "I'm ready to start exploring the resources you offer in order to consider a variety of majors, but I need some guidance on *how* to do all of that, starting now while I'm a freshman." The counselor will almost certainly see your student as a refreshing change of pace from the steady stream of second-semester sophomores who show up an hour or two before they have to register for their junior-year courses and say, "Can you help me pick a major ... by four o'clock this afternoon?!"

• ROAD MAP QUESTIONS TO ASK YOUR STUDENT •

Passions: At this point in your life, what activities might you enjoy if you were to give them a try? What topics might be interesting to study in depth? Have you considered taking an interest inventory to get some additional ideas?

Innate talents: What's your current sense of what you're good at? Have you ever thought about taking a timed abilities test to (a) confirm what you already know you're good at, and (b) uncover things you didn't know you were good at?

What matters most: Right now, what matters most to you in your life? What might matter most to you in the future career you choose (e.g., how much money you make, the lifestyle you live, the type of setting you work in)? Have you considered completing a values inventory or talking with a campus career counselor to identify values-related themes in your life?

Researching Careers

Encourage your student to begin researching careers of *potential* interest.

Why

Statistics show that there are more than twenty thousand specific job titles in the United States! How many of these jobs does your student honestly know anything about? How many of them are completely new to him?

If your student is like most college students—and people in general, for that matter—he's trying to choose a career from a box of, at best, one hundred possibilities—leaving 19,900 (probably more!) beyond his awareness, let alone his thoughtful consideration. What if one of these other careers would be a great fit for your student? What if he unknowingly passes it by?

Now you know why career exploration and research are so important.

Let's be clear: There's no way your student is going to learn about the ins and outs of twenty thousand career possibilities. He would be in college forever if he took that route! But wouldn't it be nice for him to go beyond the opposite, paltry extreme of only a hundred (or maybe far fewer!) possibilities? Wouldn't you like him to make his choice from a larger "catalog" of options?

By completing some very basic career research activities, your student will be able to do just that.

How

1. Help your student find books about various careers. He can begin his search by talking to a campus librarian and seeing if the school's library

has career exploration books. As importantly, your student should visit the school's career center and start looking through its library of books. Additionally, he can head for the local bookstore and spend some time in the "Careers" section, paging through career guides. You and your student may not know it, but several publishers produce books in the *Careers in* _____ (e.g., *Careers in Marketing*) or *Careers for* _____ *Majors* (e.g., *Careers for Psychology Majors*) genres.

2. Your student should ask the school's reference librarian for help in tracking down articles about careers of potential interest. Perhaps the local business newspaper did a story on nursing recently. Or maybe one of the thousands of *trade publications* in the United States recently ran a piece on career opportunities in biotechnology. A reference librarian can help your student get his hands on the articles he wants.

3. Encourage your student to look for web sites describing careers of interest. The widely popular search engine Google (www.google.com) is a fabulous tool for this type of research. Your student can try a Google search on the phrase "careers for finance majors," for instance, or "What can I do with a major in finance?"

4. Encourage your student to talk (in person or via phone or email) to people in careers of potential interest. You may even want to connect your student to people you know—or at least help him do so on his own. For instance, if your student reads an article about someone in a profession that intrigues him, he can email that person. He'll likely be surprised by how willing most people are to discuss their careers—in great part because most of us enjoy talking about ourselves!

5. Encourage your student to visit his school's career center and ask a counselor there to teach him additional ways to explore careers. Your student should ask for different approaches he can use. If he enjoys talking to people in person, for instance, he might benefit from directly contacting a person in a field of interest. Conversely, if your student prefers learning by reading, he'll probably get more out of finding the right books, articles, or web sites describing the career he wants to learn more about. Both of these approaches to career research are equally valid—and quite effective!

• ROAD MAP QUESTIONS TO ASK YOUR STUDENT •

Passions: What subject do you spend the most time talking about or reading about? What are its potential career possibilities?

Innate talents: Where might you apply your best—and favorite!— abilities and skills in the world of work?

What matters most: What can you envision yourself doing for forty (or more) hours a week? Does making a certain amount of money drive you? Do material possessions matter to you? Do you need to "make a difference" through your work?

dreams ... discoveries ... reflections ...
intentions ... discussions

➤━◦━➤

Mapping Your Direction

Uncovering Your Purpose
Freshman Year

"Having a purpose is the difference between
making a living and making a life."

~ TOM THISS

Now that your college student has completed her freshman year and focused on *exploration*, she's probably beginning to know who she is in a whole new way. Help her take some time now to put this newfound wisdom together by writing down what she knows to be true regarding the following questions.

She can use her responses to begin developing the bigger picture of her life—her *purpose*.

Purpose

The underlying theme of this book is centered around *purpose*. When we're truly clear about our life's purpose, we feel a sort of connectedness to greater meaning. Hopefully, your student is beginning to feel excited about her future, and that she can contribute in some way to something bigger than herself.

The questions that follow will help your student begin to uncover her purpose. Encourage her to thoughtfully ponder these questions—and the meaning of the answers that lie within.

If you can articulate your purpose, write down what you feel it is. If you can't, think about the last few times you've experienced a wonderful mood or felt totally in sync with life. What were you doing when you felt this way? Were you helping or serving others? Were you creating something new or beautiful? Were you solving a problem? What insights have you gained about your purpose? Ask these questions of yourself and try to answer as many as you can—as deeply as you can. You may not be able to answer them all or even very many, but at least you will have begun the process of asking and reflecting so that, at some point, you can answer these questions with certainty.

Here are two more questions you should contemplate:

- Are you on course with your purpose?
- Are you learning more about your purpose?

Dreams—Life's Destinations

This next set of questions is about your student's dreams. Your student may or may not want to share these thoughts with you right now, but encourage him to write them down. And when he does feel like sharing these thoughts with you, be ready to listen.

Where is it you want to go, with whom, and doing what at this time in your life? What kind of life do you want to be engaged in right now? Does that life align with "what matters most" to you?

Discoveries

Encourage your student to think about the events from her life that have led to wonderful discoveries, and to then answer the questions that follow.

Scenic highways: Write about the "scenic highways" of your freshman year—that is, what went well and the exciting events that spoke directly to your heart. What has been revealed to you about your abilities, skills, interests, and values? What has been revealed to you about who you're becoming?

We all have roadblocks that set us back or even derail us. Your student will too, since he's at a point in his life when he'll have many ups and downs. If you can help him view these roadblocks as learning opportunities, he will begin to learn a process he can use throughout his life whenever he runs into difficulty. So help your student reflect upon his roadblocks until he can comfortably deal with them and let go of the emotions attached to them. Encourage your student to write his reflections in response to the questions the follow.

Roadblocks and speed bumps: Write about the "roadblocks" and "speed bumps" you encountered this past year—your problems and struggles, big and small. How do they relate to your dreams and your future? What have you learned about yourself? Do you have any gut feelings about what it all means? What are these gut feelings?

Reflections

Reflecting on life in general helps us understand more clearly what we need to do to achieve our goals. It also helps us look over and feel good about what we've accomplished. So encourage your student to reflect upon—and then write about—the question below.

What are your deepest thoughts—the ones that are very personal and private? Take at least ten minutes to write freely about the dreams you currently have for your future.

Intentions

Your student can keep moving by setting a goal to take action on what she's discovering about herself and the world of work. The following activity will help her do just that.

Set your course: What actions will you commit to that will move you toward your dreams? Reread the lists of *academic* and *experiential* activities from freshman year and highlight the ones that are most important for you to pursue. Do you need to set a deadline for when you want to have these tasks completed? If so, create a timeline below.

Document at least two commitments you're willing to make to yourself and think about the time it will take to actually complete these activities. Record the date you want each of them completed:

Commitment one: _____

Completion date: _____

Commitment two: _____

Completion date: _____

It's important for your student to have small successes along the way. He can have those successes by developing daily intentions. So help him set up his days for success by prompting him to do the following exercise.

Daily intentions: What activities can you commit to each day to move your dreams ahead (e.g., attending classes, studying, talking with mentors, journaling your thoughts, reading through portions of your journal)?

Discussion and Dialogue

Research shows that knowledge stays with us longer if we engage in actively learning it and then reflect on it and discuss it with someone. So encourage your student to discuss his life dreams, difficulties, and successes with someone he feels knows him well. This may be you or another adult who has a special place in your student's life. The important thing is for your student to have someone to talk to regularly.

The questions below are ones your student should ask to really think clearly about who he feels he can rely on for this ongoing task.

Creating your support system: Who in your life understands you best? Who supports you through thick and thin? With whom do you feel socially adept and confident? Who do you trust to help you uncover your life's purpose? Write down the names of these people and set up a regular time to discuss your life with each of them.

Mapping Your Direction

Your student will want to forge a new path, if necessary. The next set of questions will help her determine what that new path might look like.

Looking back over your freshman-year discoveries, are there any new road maps you need to create? Do you need to check something out by taking a quick detour? What do you need to do to get going in this new direction?

_____

_____

_____

_____

_____

_____

_____

_____

_____

_____

_____

_____

_____

_____

_____

_____

_____

Sophomore Year

Examination

Introduction

Congratulations—your student has successfully completed her first year of college! If she's taken the time to start exploring major and career possibilities, she's in a good place right now. Her next step is to take stock of what she's learned so far about her passions, innate talents, and what matters most to her and to then critically examine her experiences, potential majors, and, ultimately, career possibilities in significant depth.

As a sophomore, your student will start taking courses in her potential major to gauge whether that major is a good fit for her. She'll meet regularly with academic advisors and career counselors, and begin talking with professors and other students about potential majors. She'll also learn to research internship opportunities as well as companies/organizations she might want to work for in the future. She'll start obtaining impressive experience, too, through leadership opportunities and part-time jobs. Your student may even decide to take advantage of a study abroad experience. And she'll continue developing her resumé and, eventually, complete at least one *mock interview* (i.e., a practice interview).

During the sophomore year, you'll find that your student feels more at home when she's at school. She'll start figuring out who she is and how that relates to her future. She'll be challenged to learn about herself through successes as well as bumps in the road. In the end, she'll have a deeper understanding of her place in the world and how she can fulfill her life's purpose—at least in part—through her work.

If, at first glance, the tasks and experiences of the sophomore year seem similar to the first-year activities, you're right ... to a degree. But as a sophomore, your student will be asked to complete some new activities and take the familiar ones further than before. For example, we asked your student during her first year to get involved in a campus organization. This year, we encourage her to consider taking on a minor leadership role in that organization. Indeed, through each "year" of this book, your student will build upon the activities of *The College to Career Road Map*—so that by the end of college, your student will be ready to pursue the best career for who she has become.

Parent/Student Road Map Activities

Review Your History

No person's life path—including her career—is linear, and that's OK! Encourage your student to pursue what really motivates her at this time in her life, knowing it will all probably change and evolve in the years ahead.

• PARENT TIP •

Now that your student has one year of college under her belt, take some time to assess your involvement with

her—and how that feels to her. Think back to how involved (or perhaps uninvolved) your parents were with *you in making career decisions. How did you feel about it? Share your thoughts with your student.*

Now ask your student to review the past year and describe how the interaction between the two of you felt. Was it balanced? Are there any adjustments that need to be made? (Note: You'll already have some idea about the answers to these questions by re-examining how much your student consulted you on various topics over the past year.) How has your student responded to your involvement?

Here's an activity that will help you make this important point. Have your student write an autobiographical summary of important events from the different stages of her life. How did each event impact her and change her? What did your student learn from these events? Encourage her to write down every key event she remembers from:

- Early childhood
- Elementary school
- Middle school
- High school

Discuss these events with her. As you listen, add what you've noticed about your student during the various phases of her life. Has she been outgoing or more reflective? Does she love to read or complete puzzles or spend time outdoors? Has she consistently had a few close friends or has she instead had a wide circle of friends? Has she spent more time doing specific activities during each of these life stages? Which events do you recall having a significant impact on her?

Next, discuss the following questions with your student. Again, be sure to listen carefully and fully.

- What do you know about yourself through looking back over the stages of your life? What patterns do you see?

  _____

  _____

  _____

  _____

  _____

- Is there something you used to do that you really enjoyed that you no longer enjoy now? What happened? Did someone or something influence you in a way that made you stop? Would you like to investigate this change a little more?

  _____

  _____

  _____

  _____

  _____

- Looking back over your life so far, what do you think will be ultra-important to you when you're choosing a career?

  _____

  _____

  _____

  _____

  _____

Assess Your Student's Talents

Encourage your student to look at the following ability areas and conduct a brief assessment of himself. Begin by asking him what he sees as his natural talents (using the list below). Then add your own observations. The idea here is to help your student identify—and perhaps even acknowledge—the skills that come naturally to him.

- **Spatial understanding**: It's easy for you to work with things—architecture, engineering, puzzles, etc.

- **Kinesthetic awareness**: You're naturally coordinated; you're a good athlete or you're adept at dancing, etc.

- **Numerical ability:** You have a gift for remembering numbers and details easily.

- **Intuition:** You have the ability to sense something; you just know it to be true and it turns out to indeed be true.

• P A R E N T   T I P •

Don't be surprised if your student has a completely different memory than you do about certain experiences. We all process things differently— so our respective "realities" can often be widely divergent.

- **Creative thinking:** You can create something beautiful—self-expression through writing, music, art, etc.

- **Problem solving/analysis:** You can organize facts to draw conclusions.

- **Premonition:** You feel what might happen next and project possibilities that actually end up happening.

- **Memory:** You remember phone numbers or street addresses well, or pick up on vocabulary or languages easily, or remember how to get somewhere after having driven there only once.

- **Social intelligence:** You can read people easily. You get along well with people. You have an inner sense of someone's emotions.

- **Communication:** You're naturally comfortable speaking with others.

You know how to communicate your thoughts in a way people can understand with ease.

- **Interpersonal abilities:** You have a natural sense of what makes people comfortable and you put that ability into action when you interact with others.

(Note: Be sure that you, too, complete this activity. It's good to point out your own strengths and weaknesses so that your student understands he doesn't need to have perfect abilities in all areas of his life.)

How does your student use these innate talents? Encourage him to write about each in the spaces below. What careers might fit these innate talents? Brainstorm some ideas with your student.

Spatial understanding:

_____

_____

Kinesthetic awareness:

_____

_____

Numerical ability:

_____

_____

Intuition:

_____

_____

Creative thinking:

_____

_____

Problem solving/analysis:

_____

_____

Premonition:

_____

_____

Memory:

_____

_____

Social intelligence:

_____

_____

Communication:

_____

_____

Interpersonal abilities:

_____

_____

Adapted from The Pathfinder, _Nicholas Lore (Fireside, 1998)_

Assessing What Your Student "Knows":
How Was the Knowledge Acquired?

Is your student's roommate a reliable source of career information? Probably not. Friends, movies, and television generally aren't great career resources either. But it isn't at all unusual for a college student to choose a career based on what a friend suggests or what she saw on last week's episode of *CSI: Miami*.

• P A R E N T   T I P •

You aren't an expert in every career field (no one is!)—
and both you and your student need to acknowledge that. Indeed, you might well be misinformed about a particular career. That might lead you to discourage your student from a particular career, believing there are "no jobs" in that particular area when in fact that simply isn't true. So if you really don't know something, say so. Then focus on finding reliable information elsewhere— and teach your student to do the same.

So encourage your student to be skeptical where career information is concerned, and teach her how to be discerning when it comes to who and what she'll listen to as she gathers career information. Tell your student to be especially careful about "job outlook" forecasts—since forecasts, after all, are *predictions* and not facts.

There are two wonderful tools your student (and you) can use during her career exploration and decision-making activities:

- **Inquiry and critical evaluation**—questioning and research that helps her understand herself better.

- **Exploration**—putting the inquiry and critical evaluation into action.

Have your student choose one career area she's interested in exploring in some depth. Ask her the following questions about it:

- What do you know about this area right now?
- How did you get this knowledge? Who/what were your sources of information?

• How reliable are these sources of information?

If your student discovers she's relying on sources that aren't very good, challenge her to seek out better ones! That way, she'll make *informed* career decisions.

• PARENT TIP •

Ask your student questions that expand her thinking. Help her see possibilities rather than limitations. For example, if she wants to be a writer but she says there are "no jobs" in that field, question her about how she came to that conclusion. How does she know this belief is true? Help her research writing careers by encouraging her to read about them or talk to professional writers. Make sure your student doesn't stop dreaming because of what she thinks she "knows." Instead, encourage her to actively seek out the facts and fully explore every possibility

Give Your Student a Good "SWOT"

Have your student spend some time identifying (and writing down) his perceived *strengths* and *weaknesses*, using the instructions below.

Strengths
Write down your abilities and skills, special knowledges (e.g., knowing how to carve, being able to speak Spanish), and values as well as your strongest interests.

_____

_____

_____

_____

_____

_____

Weaknesses

What are your challenges? Where do you lack experience or knowledge? Write down your perceived weak points as they might relate to your future career. What fields do you think you should avoid? Why?

_____

_____

_____

_____

_____

_____

• PARENT TIP •

It's critical for you to be fully present through listening during this activity. Try to refrain from interjecting your opinions. The goal here is to understand how your student perceives his strengths and weaknesses.

Now, have your student look at what he's written and pinpoint where he might have *opportunities* because of his experiences, special knowledge, interests, skills, and innate talents. Have him honestly assess potential *threats* as well: What might hold your student back? What obstacles might he have to overcome to achieve his career goals?

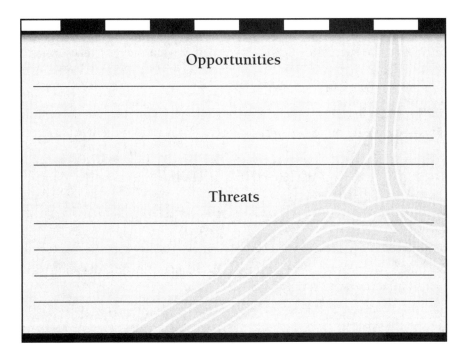

Once your student has completed his personal SWOT (**S**trengths-**W**eaknesses-**O**pportunities-**T**hreats) analysis, discuss the following questions with him:

• How can you capitalize on your *strengths* and *opportunities*?
• How can you minimize or overcome your *weaknesses* and *threats*?

~Adapted from Association Expertise, Inc.

It's *Both* What You Know *and* Who You Know!

You've undoubtedly heard the phrase, "It's not what you know, it's who you know." The reality, however, is that it's *both* what you know *and* who you know. So encourage your student to build quality relationships with other people—particularly people working in careers of potential interest. But don't forget to remind your student that her knowledge, skills, and experiences are equally important.

Working together with your student, develop a list of local people who are in a career that interests her. Encourage her to contact these professionals to see if they'd be willing to discuss their careers informally—over coffee, perhaps. What does someone (like your student, perhaps!) need to know in order to be successful in this career? And what sorts of relationships does someone (like your student, perhaps!) need to build and maintain in order to be successful in this field?

The best way for your student to uncover the answers to these key questions—and many more—is to talk to people who are in the trenches.

Academic Activities

• CONTINUING TASKS •

Encourage your student to continue using her general education *core courses* to take a wide variety of classes (see p. 18).

• NEW TASKS •

Working with a Campus Career Counselor
Encourage your student to work with a campus career counselor to explore careers, potential majors, and his unique abilities and skills.

Why
The vast majority of the careers that exist in the world of work are broader than any one college major. Indeed, in most cases your student can choose one of many majors in order to pursue a particular career path. For example, he can major in anything from English or history to biology or engineering and still eventually become an attorney (after law school, of course!).

Some careers do have a specific academic path. Becoming an actuary, for instance, requires either a math degree or an actuarial science degree. And if your student wants to become a certified public accountant (CPA), he'll need an accounting degree to prepare himself for the CPA exam.

All these options! That's why your student's most important task at this point is to understand the variety of career options that fit him—before he actually settles on a major. He needs to look extensively at what's out there. So encourage him to tap the expertise of the campus professionals around him who want (and who are paid, through tuition dollars!) to help your student choose the best-fitting major and career path. There's absolutely *no* reason for your student to tackle this process on his own.

• PARENT TIP •

If your student has already chosen his major, he'll still want to continue exploring career possibilities connected to that major and confirm that his choice is a good fit. Every major opens up many doors to various careers—sometimes careers that your student has never even heard of.

So encourage your student to work with a campus career counselor to clarify the reasons why his chosen major and career path make sense for him. You don't want your student to find out during his senior year that his major really doesn't mesh well with who he is.

You also don't want your student to feel pressure about making a choice without really understanding how that choice aligns with his passions, skills and abilities, and values. Does your student feel like he was pressured to choose the major he's selected? Then help him reassess—now—how this decision might impact his life later. Is he willing to live with this choice for at least a few years after he graduates? Does he feel he had enough information to make an informed choice, or does he need to go back and educate himself more thoroughly?

How

1. Your student can call or stop by his school's career center to set up an appointment with a career counselor there. Depending on the size of your student's school, the career center may have anywhere from one counselor to a dozen or more. If your student has a choice of counselors to see, he can try to meet with one who specializes in helping first- and second-year students. Remember: The career center is as interested in connecting your student with the right person as *you* are!

2. At his meeting with the career counselor, your student can ask about the key skills and abilities he'll need to succeed in his career areas of interest. He can also ask about the types of careers he'll be able to pursue with each of the majors he's looking at. Keep your expectations realistic here, and encourage your student to do the same: The career counselor isn't going to be able to haul out a list of a hundred specific job titles for every major at the school. But he/she will most certainly be able to teach your student how to research career options on his own. And in many cases, campus career centers do indeed have data on the types of jobs landed by various graduates (with various majors) from their schools. (They gather this information by surveying recent graduates a few months after graduation and compiling the results into a *placement report* that can then be used by other students ... like your student. Your student should definitely ask about any placement report[s] that might be available to him.)

3. Your student can ask his career counselor to help him assess each career possibility in terms of other key variables as well—such as his interests and passions, his personality, his values (i.e., what's important to him in a future career), the future *predicted* job market for people in those careers, and his personal and professional goals.

4. Once your student is done brainstorming with his career counselor, he can narrow his list of possible careers down to two or three broad career areas. That's good enough ... for now! Then your student can start looking at the potential majors that would prepare him for these careers. *But remember: Your student can always change his mind later if he wants/needs to!* (And he most certainly won't be alone if he does!)

• ROAD MAP QUESTIONS TO ASK YOUR STUDENT •

Passions: Is there a career field you've always dreamed about? Is there an academic subject/discipline that truly excites you? How does this knowledge tie in with your eventual choices of an academic major and career path?

Innate talents: What are you naturally good at doing? Could you do it for a living? Why or why not? (If *not* … are you certain your assessment is accurate? How do you know?)

What matters most: Are there things you do that seem like they're probably a part of your life's purpose? What are they? How could you tie them into your choice of an academic major? a career?

Meeting with the Academic Advisor

Encourage your student to meet with her academic advisor to explore potential majors that fit with the career areas she's considering.

Why

At most four-year colleges and universities, your student will be required to formally choose her academic major at the end of her sophomore year so that she can register for courses in that major starting junior year. So at some point during your student's sophomore year, she'll have to switch gears and move from full-fledged major *exploration* to major *decision making.*

The step in between these two activities: narrowing down her major choices so that she is seriously considering two to four majors (instead of every major at her school!), from which she'll choose one (or two if she decides to double-major). You can talk to your student about making sure the major she chooses helps her build the skills and acquire the knowledge necessary to reach success in her chosen career. (Note: Keep in mind that your student's major doesn't *limit* her career path; rather, it enhances her path. It's only one component of your student's preparation to enter a particular career.)

Your student's academic advisor will help her understand the requirements of particular careers and majors and how they intersect. Advisors have specific knowledge about the school's major, degree, and institutional requirements. For example, some majors require students to complete a prescribed set of courses before they can apply to the major. But in other cases, your student can simply declare her major and complete the required coursework before she graduates.

How

1. Early in the first semester of her sophomore year (or sooner if she's so inclined!), your student should contact her academic advisor and set up a meeting with him/her. Your student should tell her advisor that she wants to use the meeting for the specific purpose

If your student has already declared a major, she should use this meeting with her academic advisor to make sure she's on track for completing all the requirements for that major.

of beginning to narrow down her major options. Your student should also let her advisor know that her goal at this point is to get the number of options down to a manageable level—perhaps somewhere between two and four legitimate possibilities.

2. At the advising meeting, your student can discuss the careers and majors she's explored so far and which of them interest her the most. She can get her advisor's sense of the key skills and abilities she'll need to succeed in each of these careers and majors. Does your student have these skills and abilities—or could she at least develop them?

3. Your student can discuss specific degree requirements with her advisor so that she understands what's required to obtain a degree in a particular major.

• ROAD MAP QUESTIONS TO ASK YOUR STUDENT •

Passions: Do each of the majors you're considering truly fit *your* interests? Do you really enjoy the subject matter you'll be studying in each of them?

Innate talents: Will you be able to perform well in the classes offered in these majors? How do you know?

What matters most: Will you be studying something that matters to you in these majors, and that will allow you to live the life you want to live (whatever that may entail!) after you graduate? How do you know?

Choosing a Minor

Talk with your student about exploring minors that might complement the majors he's still strongly considering.

Why

Your student can't major in everything, but if he's like most students he's interested in more than one subject or discipline. So encourage your student to explore a *minor* area of study to complement the major area of study he ultimately chooses (even though most schools don't require a minor for graduation). Not only will a minor diversify your student's academic experience; it will also give him a more compelling combination of knowledge and skills than he might otherwise gain, making him a better candidate for future internships and jobs.

How

1. Your student has already been exploring potential majors, most of which he will *not* end up pursuing. Now, encourage your student to talk to his academic advisor or a career counselor to get his/her ideas on which of these academic disciplines, if any, might make for a good minor given the two to four majors your student is still considering at this point.

2. Encourage your student to consult the department web sites for each of the minors on his list. What courses will he need to take for each minor, and how many credits are involved?

3. Just as he did after exploring majors, your student can come up with a list of two to four *minors* he'd like to seriously think about. That's good enough … for now! And again, he can always change his mind later if he wants/needs to.

4. Keep in mind that the minor your student chooses isn't nearly as crucial as the major he selects—at least in the eyes of most employers.

Your student has a bit more flexibility where his minor is concerned; there is less pressure on him to pick the "perfect" discipline. On the scale of life's decisions, the minor your student chooses is, well, a comparatively minor decision!

• ROAD MAP QUESTIONS TO ASK YOUR STUDENT •

Passions: Is there an academic field you like that you can't or won't pursue as a major?

Innate talents: Is there an academic field (other than your major) that you're good at? Is there a particular skill you can build through a minor that would be valuable in your career areas of interest?

What matters most: Is there an academic field that means enough to you that you'll devote several courses to studying it?

Beginning Major-Course Studies

Encourage your student to sign up for an introductory course (or two) in the top major she's considering. (Ideally, she'll take this course no later than second semester of sophomore year.)

Why

Your student can read a lot about the top major she's considering, and she can even talk to students and professors from that major to get their ideas on what the major is all about. But your student won't get a true feel for the major unless and until she takes an introductory course or two within that major's academic department. She needs to experience the major firsthand—its concepts, its professors, and its students—if she wants to have a true sense of how well (or not) it fits *her*.

How

1. Unless this task was covered during a previous session, your student can set up a meeting with her academic advisor shortly before she'll be registering for her courses for the upcoming semester.

2. Your student should ask her advisor to help her choose not only a few courses that count toward her core requirements, but also at least one

If your student has already declared a major, she can take introductory courses in both semesters of her sophomore year. Why? To get a real feel for the major she's chosen. Your student can take the time to reflect upon whether her expectations are in line with what *she originally thought this major would offer. If your student has a hunch that there are still other majors she'd like to explore, then there's no better time than now to start exploring. She still has plenty of time to change her major to one that truly fits.*

course from the top major she's considering. Your student can select her potential-major course first, then choose and schedule her remaining courses around that one.

3. Your student should also choose a backup course in her potential-major department in case she can't get into her first-choice course. Your student can even ask her advisor to help her develop a complete back-up schedule—built around this backup potential-major course—just in case her first-choice potential-major course falls through. One way or the other, your student has *got* to get at least one course from her top potential major into her schedule for the upcoming semester.

• ROAD MAP QUESTIONS TO ASK YOUR STUDENT •

Passions: How do you feel about the potential-major course you've chosen with respect to your interests? Is the course what you thought it would be? Why or why not?

Innate talents: How are you doing in the potential-major course you picked? Do you think you can handle the work involved in the major you're considering?

What matters most: Does the subject matter of this potential-major course grab you? Will you be able to apply what you're learning in a real-world career after graduation—so that you can live the life you want to live (whatever that may entail!)?

Evaluating Academic Progress

Encourage your student to meet with his academic advisor to critically evaluate his academic progress.

Why

Your student pretty much *has* to meet with his academic advisor at least once a semester, if only to get him/her to sign off on a proposed schedule of courses for the next semester. If your student stops there, though, he won't

If your student has already declared a major, meeting with his academic advisor is key to staying on task and assessing how he's doing academically. That way, nothing will slip through the cracks and your student will be much more likely to graduate on time.

really get to know his advisor very well—nor will the advisor get to know him. Moreover, your student won't be able to tap his advisor's knowledge of the school's academic programs and corresponding post-graduation career opportunities.

If, on the other hand, your student sets up a second meeting to review his academic progress—perhaps around mid-semester or shortly thereafter—(a) he'll stand out in his advisor's mind as a student who takes his college experience seriously, and (b) he'll become one of the few advisees the advisor actually proac-

tively collaborates with—and not just a vaguely familiar face who shows up once a semester to have his course schedule approved during a two-minute, largely artificial interaction.

How

1. Your student can set up a meeting with his academic advisor a week or two after his midterm exams are done. Your student should ask his advisor for help with reviewing his academic progress so far, including how he's moving toward his degree and graduation requirements.

2. Your student should look at his cumulative grade point average (GPA) so far. If he's struggling, he should ask his advisor to give him the name of a key person or office on campus that can help him raise his grades. Does the school have a Learning Center (or similarly named office), for example, or an office where your student can work with a tutor for the course that's driving him nuts?

3. Your student should step away from his grades momentarily and ask his advisor for guidance on identifying which courses he has *enjoyed* the most so far (and why), as well as which ones he's enjoyed the least (and why). Your student can also ask for help with pinpointing key likes and dislikes that have emerged from his coursework to date.

• ROAD MAP QUESTIONS TO ASK YOUR STUDENT •

Passions: Do you find that you always study for a particular course first? last? Why do you think you operate this way?

Innate talents: Are you more successful in a particular course? What skills and abilities do you possess that make it easier to do well in this course?

What matters most: Do any of your courses fit with your heart? Do any of them seem especially meaningful to you? Why?

Preparing for Studying Abroad

Encourage your student to firm up any plans she has for studying abroad later in her sophomore year, during a J-term (January term), during her junior year, or during an upcoming summer.

Why

Studying abroad is one of the best ways your student can gain exposure to the world around her and learn about a culture that's different from her own—both experiences that employers value highly in new college graduates (see p. 31 of Freshman Year), especially in our increasingly global world economy and job market. If an employer knows your student can work well with people (e.g., clients, colleagues) from another culture— and perhaps even live *within* that culture without any major problems—

that employer is much more likely to hire *your student* vs. another recent grad who doesn't have this background.

How

1. If she hasn't already done so, your student can visit her school's Study Abroad office or department and ask for general information on study abroad opportunities offered through the school.

2. Encourage your student to meet individually with an advisor in the Study Abroad office, or to see if there are any upcoming introductory sessions for students who are interested in potentially studying abroad.

3. Your student can also ask her academic advisor, her professors, a campus career counselor, or her friends if they know anyone who is currently studying abroad or who has done so in the past. Encourage your student to contact some of these study abroad veterans to get the inside scoop on what the experience is really like.

4. Encourage your student to check out the web sites of organizations like the Council on International Educational Exchange (www.ciee.org) and the Institute of International Education (www.iie.org) to learn more about study abroad possibilities.

5. Help your student decide which study abroad experiences she wants to pursue and complete the appropriate paperwork for it. Your student will need to send in her applications, with applicable fees, long before the application deadline to ensure she'll be considered.

6. Once your student knows where she'll be studying abroad, she'll need to work closely with her academic advisor and/or the school's study abroad coordinator to make key preparations ahead of time—e.g., where she'll live in the host country, what she'll study and where, places where she can look for a job while she's there, and people she can contact for help once she's in the country.

7. During her study abroad experience, your student should keep a detailed journal or diary of her daily activities. What new skills is she learning? What surprises or excites her about this new culture? What is your student struggling with? Your student should keep track of it all—not only for her own trip down memory lane years from now, but also for resumé development and interviewing purposes once she's back home!

• ROAD MAP QUESTIONS TO ASK YOUR STUDENT •

Passions: Do you enjoy new adventures, exploring the unknown, and learning about a culture that's different—perhaps very different—from your own? Why or why not? What is it about the idea of studying abroad that appeals to you?

Innate talents: Are you able to roll with change and survive—even thrive—in a strange environment? If you study in a non-English-speaking country, do you have the foreign language skills necessary to function there on a day-to-day basis? Are you naturally adaptable, flexible, and open-minded? How well do you do when you don't know, ahead of time, what problems and issues you're going to have to deal with?

What matters most: Do you believe it's valuable, in and of itself, to understand cultures that are different from your own and, from a career perspective, to pursue a career that at least occasionally takes you outside the country? Will your time studying abroad give you experiences that are important to you and your future career aspirations?

Getting to Know One's Professors

Support your student as he expands his efforts to get to know his professors; he needs to go beyond knowing just *one* of them.

Why

The diversity among the professors at your student's school—particularly in terms of their knowledge bases and areas of expertise—is amazing. So if your student is in career and major exploration mode (which he is at this point), doesn't it make sense for him to talk to as many of his instructors as possible to learn more about their academic departments (and the potential careers he could pursue by majoring in one of those disciplines)? Why *wouldn't* your student want to be introduced to as many different ideas as possible?

How

1. What is your student's favorite course this semester? Next time your student has this class, encourage him to take a moment immediately

Getting to know his professors is an essential task for your student, whether he's declared a major or not. Professors can lend a helpful ear and give great advice. They also have real-world contacts—often alumni/ae of the school—who may be helpful to your student in some way. So getting to know a variety of professors is a fabulous way for your student to expand his knowledge about the career possibilities his chosen major offers—or even another major he hasn't yet considered.

after the class session to talk to the professor before he/she leaves the room. Your student can tell the professor that he's finding the course topics genuinely interesting, and that he's in the process of exploring what major to pursue.

2. Encourage your student to ask the professor if he/she would be willing to meet to discuss not the course per se, but what it's like to major in that course's discipline. If the professor *is* willing to meet, your student can get on his/her schedule right then and there.

3. Advise your student to go to the meeting prepared to take the lead in his discussion with the professor. When the professor invariably asks, "So…what is it that you wanted to talk about?", your student needs to be ready to say something like this: "I'm thinking about what to major in right now, and _____ is on my list of possibilities. Could you tell me a little bit about this major? What kinds of jobs do people use this major for? What skills will I learn?"

4. Your student should take a few notes on the professor's suggestions and ask him/her if there are *other* things he can do to explore the major (e.g., talking to other professors in the department, reading books, visiting web sites).

5. Encourage your student to repeat this same process with the instructors he has for *other* courses he finds interesting. All he has to do is show

genuine interest in his instructors' disciplines; invariably, those instructors will remember your student not as "just another student in one of my classes," but as one of those rare students who seems to truly care about what he's learning and why.

• ROAD MAP QUESTIONS TO ASK YOUR STUDENT •

Passions: Are there any professors you're drawn to and excited to be around because they hold your interest? What's so appealing about them?

Innate talents: Is there anything you're consistently complimented on by your professors? Do they point out to you what might not be obvious to you—that you're good at a certain something? How come you've never recognized this key skill or ability yourself? Could the same be true of other skills and abilities?

What matters most: Are you finding that your values mesh well with what you're experiencing as you talk to different professors? Why or why not?

Talking to Upperclassmen

Suggest to your student that he talk to upperclassmen in the majors he's considering.

Why

It's great whenever your student can read about a particular major in a book or on a web site. But he'll get another essential perspective by talking to the *students* who are in that major right now. Not only will these students know which courses are interesting (or not) and which professors fit your student's learning style (or not); they'll also be aware of internships their fellow students (or they themselves) are doing within the major, and perhaps even the entry-level jobs landed by their slightly older peers who have graduated from the major in the last year or two.

In short, upperclassmen in the majors your student is considering will be among your student's best sources of learning about the day-to-day realities of being in that major, as well as the future internship and job possibilities within that major.

If your student has already declared a major, talking to upperclassmen is a great way for him to connect with students who have already successfully maneuvered through many of the courses in that major. Upperclassmen may have some very helpful advice on professors' teaching styles that could help your student choose his course schedule more wisely. Upperclassmen may also know something about the major that your student doesn't, which may impact his thoughts about that major. Moreover, upperclassmen can give your student a clearer idea of what he needs to do to be successful in the major, both in and out of class.

How

1. If there are upperclassmen in any of your student's courses and that class is in a discipline of interest, encourage your student to catch one of these upperclassmen before or after class and ask if he/she would be willing to tell him a bit more about the major. What's good about it from this student's perspective? What's bad? What internships and jobs has this student heard of other students/grads landing with that major?

2. Encourage your student to go to the school's Student Organizations office or Student Activities office (or a similarly named office) to see if there are any student groups related to the majors that are of strong interest to him. For example, if your student is taking an introductory public relations course and he finds himself enjoying it, he should see if the school has a related campus organization like the Public Relations Student Society of America (www.prssa.org). If it does, encourage your student to contact one of the leaders of the group or visit its web site to see when the group meets on campus. He can then attend the group's next meeting as a prospective member who wants to learn more about the organization. Most groups welcome interested students with open arms—and their upperclass student leaders are typically glad to answer questions about the discipline associated with the group.

3. If your student lives in a residence hall or an apartment where juniors and seniors also live, encourage him to ask one or more of these upper-classmen if they happen to be majoring in the discipline your student is interested in (or if they know of *other* upperclassmen who are major-ing in that discipline). Your student can then ask these upperclassmen if they'd be willing to tell him about the major and share what they've learned about the major so far.

• ROAD MAP QUESTIONS TO ASK YOUR STUDENT •

Passions: Do the majors you're learning about seem to focus on topics and challenges you really enjoy? Will you like going to your classes, or dread it? How do you know?

Innate talents: Will you be able to perform well in the courses within these majors, academically speaking, based on what you're hearing from its upperclass students? Why or why not?

What matters most: Do the students you've talked to seem passionate about what they're studying? Is it clear that what they're studying mat-ters to them and has application in a real-world career after graduation?

Focusing on the Professors in Your Student's Potential Majors

Encourage your student to talk to professors in the majors she's considering.

Why

It's one thing for your student to get the perspective of her fellow students on particular majors of interest. (See "Talking to Upperclassmen," p. 89). But unlike her fellow undergraduates, the *professors* in the majors that inter-est your student have obviously demonstrated a significant commitment to it by studying it for years and, in most cases, earning a doctoral degree in it so they can teach it and research it at the college level. Clearly, then, profes-sors must feel very strongly about their disciplines. Your student can easily find out why—and whether she, too, might share a particular professor's passion and turn it into some sort of career someday.

Your student needs to seek professors out, for they won't come to her on the off chance she might be interested in what they have to say; she has to show her professors that she's interested in what they do and why. Usually, once your student demonstrates genuine interest in it, a professor will talk your student's ear off about his/her discipline. After all ... it's the topic he/she has committed to for the long haul.

If your student has already chosen her major, encourage her to seek out professors in that major so she can develop networking contacts for potential internships or jobs later in her college career. Who knows—one of these professors might even become a professional reference for your student someday! It's always good for your student to have a professor know her well as a person—as someone beyond just another student in his/her class—because he/she can then speak more specifically to prospective employers (or graduate/professional programs) about your student's skills, knowledge, and interests. The more specific your student's professors can be when they talk about her, the better her references will be and the more weight those references will carry when it matters most.

How

1. Once your student has a major/discipline in mind that she'd like to learn more about, she can go to her school's web site and find the link to the web site of that major's/discipline's academic department. (Generally she'll find this information under a broad heading like "Academics" or "Programs and Majors" on the campus web site's home page.)

2. Once your student is on the major's/discipline's web site, she can look for a link called "Faculty" (or something similar)—basically, the place on the site that lists the names and contact information of all faculty members within the department.

3. Coach your student to look for a professor or two who seems like he/she might be a good person to talk to given his/her biographical

information or position. Is there a professor, for example, who advises an on-campus organization for students in that major department? Is there a professor who has published papers or spoken at conferences on a topic that really grabs your student? Is there a professor who, fairly or unfairly, has a photograph that makes him/her look friendly and approachable? (Or, alternatively, is there a professor your student has heard about through the student grapevine as being friendly and enthusiastic toward students?)

4. Talk to your student about how she'd like to approach this professor to discuss the professor's discipline. Depending on your student's personality, she may be most comfortable simply stopping by the professor's office out of the blue to ask for a meeting ... or calling him/her to ask for a meeting ... or emailing him/her to ask for a meeting. *How* your student asks for a meeting with the professor doesn't matter; *that* she asks is what counts.

5. Your student can tell the professor that she's exploring the possibility of majoring in his/her discipline, but that she'd like to learn more about it before she makes her final decision. Encourage your student to ask for about twenty minutes of the professor's time so she could ask a few basic questions.

6. The vast majority of professors will gladly talk to your student about their disciplines ... if your student asks. A few, however, will decline (for various reasons). Don't be alarmed by this development—and, much more importantly, don't conclude that *all* of the professors in the department will treat your student this way ... because they won't. Instead, simply tell your student to find another professor to approach with her request. Encourage her to keep asking around until she finds a professor who's willing to chat with her.

7. During your student's chat with the professor, she should ask him/her what's good about the discipline, what's not so good, and what internships and jobs are landed by students and graduates of that particular major.

8. Your student can wrap up the meeting by asking the professor about other things she can do to learn more about the professor's discipline. Are there other people your student can talk to? books she can read? web sites she can visit?

Passions: Do the professors you've talked to exude a joy for what they do? Does their discipline speak to you, too? Why or why not?

Innate talents: Will you be able to hold your own in this major's courses, academically speaking, based on what you've heard from the professors you've talked to? How do you know?

What matters most: Do the professors you've talked to seem passionate about what they're studying and teaching? Is it clear that what they're studying and teaching matters and has application in the world of work after graduation?

Experiential Activities

• CONTINUING TASKS •

- Encourage your student to keep looking for ways to volunteer (see p. 37).
- Remind your student to continue collecting items for her career portfolio (see p. 42).

• NEW TASKS •

Pursuing a Leadership Role in a Campus Organization

Encourage your student to pursue a leadership role in at least one campus organization.

Why

It's one thing for your student to *participate* in a campus organization. But employers who hire new college graduates consistently report that they're looking for graduates who have *leadership* skills and experience. (Not convinced? Review the "soft skills" survey of employers on pp. 35-36.)

Taking on a high-level role in a student group is a natural way for your student to develop sound leadership skills—not to mention many other skills (e.g., team building, organization, conceptualizing) that will help her in her future career.

How

1. If your student is already a member of a campus organization, encourage her to ask one of its current leaders about leadership opportunities she can pursue within the group. Encourage your student to go after one of these opportunities.

2. If your student is not currently in a campus organization, encourage her to go to the school's Student Activities office or Student Organizations office (or a similarly named office) to see which groups exist at her school. She can then pick one or two that sound interesting and see if they have web sites or information blurbs in her undergraduate bulletin or student handbook. (Usually, the number of choices is amazing. Your student may be able to participate in anything from the biology club to the water ski club!) Encourage your student to contact leaders or members of these groups to see what leadership opportunities exist within them, particularly at "lower" levels.

3. If your student isn't able to land a leadership role in a campus organization at this time, encourage her to talk to the leaders of the organizations that interest her and get their advice on how she can best prepare to land a leadership position during her *junior* year.

• ROAD MAP QUESTIONS TO ASK YOUR STUDENT •

Passions: Do you like the idea of being a leader? Why or why not? Do you enjoy influencing your peers? Why or why not?

Innate talents: Are you good at being a leader? Do people naturally follow you? Do you have good interpersonal skills? How do you know?

What matters most: Do you have compassion for others? Do you enjoy improving organizations and systems for the greater good? Why or why not?

Campus Leadership Positions

Ask your student if he's explored applying for one of the unique campus leadership positions at his school.

Why

Who are the student leaders you and your student have seen at his school—Resident Assistants, Community Advisors, Admissions Ambassadors, Orientation Leaders, Alumni Ambassadors, Peer Advisors, Health Advocates, and others? They stand out on campus, don't they.

They stand out to future employers, too.

Typically these unique campus leadership positions require a tremendous amount of responsibility. The students in these roles have been selected and trained. They're also well embedded within the campus community—a situation that affords them many opportunities that other students simply don't get.

One of these unique campus leadership roles can help *your* student build sound communication, problem-solving, and critical thinking skills—and result in a solid professional reference from at least one mid-level or even high-level campus administrator.

How

1. Typically, the offices and departments that offer unique campus leadership positions are: Residence Life (Housing Services), First-Year Programs, Orientation, Admissions, Health Services, and Alumni Relations. Your student can contact these offices (or visit their web sites) to find out about the opportunities that are available, the selection process(es) for those positions, and the minimum requirements to apply.

2. If his school has a separate Leadership Office, encourage your student to ask someone there about the variety of opportunities on campus to get involved and build leadership skills. More than likely, there are leadership possibilities your student isn't even aware of … yet!

3. Usually, unique campus leadership positions are highly sought after and competitive. (That's why the students who land them are so desirable to graduate/professional school programs and prospective employers.) The process often involves several interviews (individual or group); a written application complete with essay questions; and a written reference from someone who can discuss your student's people skills, dependability, organizational skills, communication skills, and problem-solving skills.

• ROAD MAP QUESTIONS TO ASK YOUR STUDENT •

Passions: Do you enjoy leading your peers in broad-based activities? Do you have an interest in taking on significant responsibilities? Why or why not?

Innate talents: Do you have solid communication skills, problem-solving skills, and critical thinking skills—or could you develop them? Are you self-directed? How do you know?

What matters most: Do you enjoy helping others learn and develop? What value(s) do you see in being able to influence your peers?

Is Your Student's Part-Time Job Providing Learning Opportunities?

Encourage your student to assess her part-time job to ensure it's giving her solid learning opportunities. (If it isn't, discuss with your student the possibility of her finding a different part-time job.)

Why

Almost 75 percent of full-time college students work to help pay for their educational expenses, according to the U.S. Department of Education. And of those students who do work, the Department of Education says, 71 percent do so for fifteen hours a week or more.

Up until this time in your student's college career, working—in and of itself—was probably enough to be of benefit to her where her long-term career interests are concerned. But now she needs to evaluate whether she's being challenged in her job and whether that job is helping her move toward the career of her choice. A part-time job can (and should) be more than just a paycheck; it can help your student build the key skills and traits that will be sought by future employers, give her valuable experience, and help her make important contacts in the world of work.

How

1. Encourage your student to make a list of the skills and traits she's building in her current part-time job. (If she doesn't have a part-time job right now, encourage her to make a list of the skills and traits she developed in previous jobs.) Are these skills *transferable*—that is, key skills (e.g., communication, teamwork, self-motivation) she'll need to be successful in *any* career she might pursue? If so, your student can continue working to build these skills. If not, she should consider looking for another part-time job—one that will teach her these skills.

2. If your student concludes that she does indeed need to look for a different part-time job, encourage her to write down some general ideas about the type of job she'd like to get. What activities should it encompass? What would she like to try? What opportunities would challenge her to learn something new? Encourage your student to write these criteria down so she has a crystal clear picture of what her next part-time job needs to "look" like.

3. Review with your student the ideas from Freshman Year (see p. 39) on how she can look for a part-time job. That way she'll be able to track down a wide variety of opportunities using a wide variety of resources.

4. Help your student think about the following practical questions with respect to a part-time job:

   - How much do you need to be paid to earn the amount of money you need for school?
   - Where (location) must you work so you can actually get to your job each day?
   - Are you limited in any way in the type of job you can pursue? How so?

• ROAD MAP QUESTIONS TO ASK YOUR STUDENT •

Passions: Is there something you're doing (or could do) in your part-time job that would align well with your natural passions? If not, is there anything you could do to change the situation, if only slightly?

Innate talents: What are the essential skills you need to learn through your part-time job? How do you know these skills are critical to your future career success?

What matters most: Is there a company/organization you could work for that fits your most cherished values? If so, have you checked to see about part-time job openings there?

Revising the Resumé

Remind your student to revise his resumé to reflect the experiences, skills, and accomplishments he gained during freshman year and the summer following freshman year.

Why

A resumé is a living document that needs to change as your student changes and grows. It would be foolish for your student to write his resumé once and then rest on it. After all, as he progresses through his college years, he gains more and more experiences, skills, and accomplishments to brag about!

How

1. Encourage your student to make an appointment with a campus career counselor so he can work on revising his resumé.

2. Before the appointment, your student should take three sheets of paper and label them "New Experiences," "New Skills," and "New Accomplishments," respectively. (You can join him in this exercise as a way of putting yourself in his shoes.)

3. Your student should take his "New Experiences" sheet and start jotting down any new experiences he can think of that have occurred between

his freshman year and now. *Stress to your student that he should not limit himself at this point!* If something jumps into his mind—no matter how minor or insignificant it might seem—he should write it down! The idea is for him to do a "brain dump" and get everything out of his head and onto paper. Later, he and his career counselor can decide what to add to his resumé and what to leave off.

4. Encourage your student to go through the same "brain dump" exercise with his "New Skills" and "New Accomplishments" sheets. Again, *stress to your student that he should not limit himself at this point!*

5. Once your student has finished writing down everything he can think of on each of the sheets, encourage him to keep those sheets in a handy spot…just in case he thinks of other entries to add later.

6. Your student should then bring these completed sheets to his appointment with the career counselor and tell him/her that he's written down everything he can think of. Your student can then ask the counselor to help him remember or acknowledge anything he may have forgotten or disregarded.

7. With the counselor's help, your student can decide which entries to add to his resumé and which to leave off. He'll almost certainly have to do some reformatting of his resumé to accommodate the changes.

8. Once your student has finished revising his resumé, he can ask the counselor to look at the document one last time (for now, at least!) for minor revisions.

• R O A D   M A P   Q U E S T I O N S   T O   A S K   Y O U R   S T U D E N T •

Passions: Does your resumé effectively reflect what you're passionate about? How do you know?

Innate talents: Are your abilities and skills effectively highlighted on your resumé? How do you know?

What matters most: Does your resumé speak clearly about what you represent and what matters to you? How do you know?

Utilizing Informational Interviews

Advise your student to conduct *informational interview*—to research careers in more depth by not only reading about them, but talking (in person or via phone/email) to people who actually work in them.

Why

It's one thing for your student to read about a particular career in a book or on a web site, but it's quite another for her to talk to people who actually work in that career. That's what *informational interviewing* is all about.

The people who work in particular careers of interest will be able to tell your student about subtleties and nuances that books and web sites can't possibly cover. Industry insiders will also be able to describe how their specific organizations work, how they themselves chose their fields, and what they had to do to land a job.

How

1. Encourage your student to choose a field/industry or company/organization she'd like to learn more about—in depth.

2. Advise your student to ask people she already knows—relatives, professors, friends, her academic advisor, her career counselor—if they have any contacts in the field/industry or company/organization your student would like to research.

3. Perhaps one of the people your student already knows *does* identify someone your student could talk to. If that happens, encourage your student to ask the acquaintance if he/she would be willing to contact the third person on your student's behalf—to feel out whether it would be OK for *your student* to get in touch with this third person directly. (Note: It almost always *is* OK!) This strategy will help your student significantly because it will prepare the third person for your student's initial contact later; that way your student won't be contacting this third person out of the blue, as a *complete* stranger.

4. Perhaps one of the people your student already knows *does not* identify someone your student could talk to. If that happens, encourage your student to talk to a campus career counselor to generate informational interview leads. It may take a bit of time and investigation,

but together the counselor and your student will be able to find at least one potential contact (and probably far more than one!).

5. Once your student has identified a person she wants to talk to, help her decide *how* to approach that person in a way that best fits her personality. If your student is more outgoing and extraverted, for example, she might be most comfortable giving the person a call. But if your student is more reserved and introverted, she might feel better writing to or emailing the person instead. *Encourage your student to use whatever approach works best for her!*

6. In her approach call/email/letter, your student should tell the person who she is, where she's going to school, and what she's trying to learn (e.g., "I'm trying to find out more about the ____ field"). She should also reassure the person that she's *not* interested in hitting him/her up for a job. Rather, she's simply looking for information and advice.

7. Your student should ask the person if he/she would be willing to meet for thirty minutes to answer a few basic questions about his/her field/industry or company/organization.

8. The vast majority (80 percent or better) of the time, the person will be glad to meet with your student. If that's the case this time, your student can go ahead and set up an appointment. (Note: If the person is unwilling or unable to meet with your student, she can politely thank him/her for his/her time and approach another person instead.)

9. Before your student's meeting, encourage her to write down the basic questions she'd like to ask the interviewee. She can use common sense to come up with most of her questions (e.g., "What do you do in your job?"), but she can get additional ideas from a counselor (or a book) at the campus career center.

10. Encourage your student to dress nicely for the informational interview, to show up on time, and to greet the interviewee with a warm "hello" and a solid introductory handshake. If it so happens that your student will be meeting the person at a coffee shop, restaurant, etc., your student should *insist* on buying!

11. Encourage your student to jot down a few notes during the meeting and keep track of any new questions that pop into her head.

12. Advise your student to stick firmly to the thirty minutes she's asked for. She should be prepared to close the meeting once those thirty minutes have elapsed. However, if the interviewee insists that it's OK to talk a little longer, encourage your student to go ahead and do so.

13. Once the informational interview is over, your student should shake the interviewee's hand once again, thank him/her profusely, and then go home and *immediately* write a thank-you note to him/her. Remind your student to be sure the note is in the mail within twenty-four hours of the meeting.

• ROAD MAP QUESTIONS TO ASK YOUR STUDENT •

Passions: After talking with someone in a career that interests you, has your interest in the career grown? decreased? Does what you learned about the career match up with what you've learned by reading about that career?

Innate talents: Do you believe you'll be able to perform successfully in the career you learned about in your informational interview? Why or why not? Are you more confident in your ability to handle this type of job? less confident? Why?

What matters most: Will you be able to do and achieve most of the things that are important to you by pursuing this particular career? How do you know? How did your informational interviewee help you affirm (or disaffirm) this conclusion?

Creating an "Internship/Co-op Possibilities" Binder

Encourage your student to create an "Internship/Co-op Possibilities" binder by researching internship and co-op possibilities.

Why

At some point during his college career (the sooner the better!), your student should complete at least one internship or co-op experience. Why? Well, a few schools (to their great credit) require it. But there's a much more important reason too: Today's employers expect your student to

• FACT •

- *In the* 2005 Graduating Student & Alumni Survey *conducted by the National Association of Colleges and Employers (a trade association for college/university career services professionals and employers who hire new college graduates), 39.4 percent of the 750+ students surveyed said they'd completed at least one internship during college, and 8.1 percent said they'd completed at least one co-op experience.*

- *In the* 2005 College Graduation Survey *conducted by Monster TRAK (the college student/recent graduate web site of online job site Monster), 59 percent of the nearly 11,000 college students surveyed said they'd completed at least one internship during college.*

- *In the* 2005 College Graduate Career Survey *conducted by Experience (a career web site for college students/recent graduates), 67 percent of the 6,500 students surveyed said they'd completed at least one internship.*

come out of college with at least *some* hands-on experience in his chosen field. If he doesn't, he'll have difficulty competing against a substantial number of his peers—who *will* have internship and/or co-op experience.

If your student chooses not to bother with an internship or a co-op, he'll be competing for an entry-level job with students and recent grads who *have* done internships and/or co-ops (often more than one!). And that contest won't last long—for your student will likely be *unable* to effectively compete given his comparative lack of experience.

There are many internship and co-op opportunities available to your student. But he probably won't pursue any of them until *next* year (i.e., junior year). That's why it's so important for him to start keeping track of internships and/or co-ops he learns about *this* year (i.e., sophomore year).

By simply printing out information about these opportunities and keeping the materials in his possession, your student will be able to effectively do just that—so that next year (or sooner if he chooses), he'll have solid leads on internships or co-ops he can try to *land*.

How

1. Here are several specific ways your student can begin researching future internship and co-op possibilities:

   - He can visit his school's career center (or its web site) and read the internship and co-op listings the center has obtained from specific organizations.

   - He can check out a college-oriented career web site like Monster-TRAK (www.monstertrak.com), Experience (www.experience.com), CollegeGrad (www.collegegrad.com), or CollegeRecruiter (www.college recruiter.com) and look for internship and co-op listings there.

   - He can go to his campus library or a nearby bookstore and look through one of the many printed internship directories that are on the market (published annually by companies like Princeton Review and Peterson's). (Note: At the bookstore, your student will find such books in the "Careers" or "College Guides" section.)

   - He can talk to his professors and his fellow students and ask them where current and previous students from his school/department have done internships or co-ops in the past. (Note: Employers often prefer hiring new interns/co-op students from the same schools/departments where they've had success doing so in the past. Your student can take advantage of this phenomenon!)

   - He can talk to a counselor at his school's career center (particularly if the center has an *internship coordinator* or similarly titled person on staff). Your student can ask where previous students from his school have interned or done co-ops in the past.

   - He can directly approach organizations that interest him and ask (by phone or email) whether those organizations have internship or co-op opportunities for college students. If they do, your student can ask how he can learn more about those possibilities.

2. As your student comes across internship and co-op possibilities of interest, encourage him to write down key details about them in a note-book—or, better yet, to photocopy or print the information he finds and keep it all in a three-ring binder labeled "Internship/Co-op Possibilities." Your student will be coming back to this critical information just a few months from now (or sooner)—so he should make sure it's well organized and easy to find!

• ROAD MAP QUESTIONS TO ASK YOUR STUDENT •

Passions: What career or field are you drawn to explore in depth—and in a very practical, hands-on kind of way—by working in it for a few months via an internship or a co-op? Why?

Innate talents: What career or field might be one in which you'll excel—or in which you may excel if given the opportunity to try it via an internship or a co-op? Why?

What matters most: What career or field might be one in which you do work that aligns well with your values (i.e., what's important to you)? Why?

Developing a "Dream Companies" Binder

Encourage your student to develop a "Dream Companies" binder by researching companies/organizations she thinks she *might* want to work for someday.

Why

At some point during the upcoming months, your student will need to narrow her choices to a few companies/organizations she wants to focus on for her internship, co-op, and, eventually, job search activities. (She can't work everywhere, after all!) So this is the time to encourage your student to begin doing some initial research on companies/organizations that interest her.

At this point, your student doesn't have to know everything there is to know about various companies/organizations; but it is important for her to know *something* about the places she may want to approach later about an internship, a co-op, or an entry-level job. By organizing this type of information from the start—and hanging onto it in a safe place—your student will be able to draw upon it throughout the rest of her college career and, especially, during her future job search(es).

How

1. Suggest to your student that she visit the web sites of companies/organizations that interest her. What do these companies/organizations do, generally speaking? What do their values seem to be? Is there any evidence that they have big plans for future expansion or growth? And do they appear to offer internship, co-op, or entry-level job opportunities?

2. Encourage your student to start reading a daily newspaper (in print or online) so she can keep an eye out for mentions of her target companies/organizations. What are various media outlets writing about "her" companies/organizations?

3. Encourage your student to go to the campus library and ask a reference librarian there to show her how to use online databases like Lexis/Nexis and ProQuest. That way she can search for articles about "her" companies/organizations in trade publications and other off-the-beaten- path media outlets. What are these publications writing about "her" companies/organizations?

4. Encourage your student to ask her professors, her friends, her academic advisor, a campus career counselor, and anyone else she can think of if they know anything about "her" target companies/organizations. For example, does one of the counselors at the campus career center regularly interact with a recruiter from one of your student's target companies/organizations? If so, what has the counselor learned about the company/organization through his/her interactions with the recruiter?

5. As your student finds information about particular companies/organizations that resonate with her, encourage her to keep that information in a "Dream Companies" binder. Tell your student to make copies of the information and organize it by company. She'll be able to use this information later in her college career—when she begins interviewing for an internship, a co-op, or a job.

Passions: Which companies/organizations are doing or making things that really grab your attention in a positive way? What, specifically, is so intriguing about these organizations?

Innate talents: As you research companies/organizations, what patterns or trends do you see in terms of the skills/abilities required for working in those companies/organizations? What *hard* skills (e.g., writing, balancing a ledger) and *soft* skills (e.g., working well with other people, taking initiative) are most frequently mentioned as being critical to success?

What matters most: Which companies/organizations seem to value the things you value (or most of them, at least)? And which companies/organizations offer career opportunities that will allow you to live the life you want to live after graduation (whatever that may entail)?

Mock Interviews

Advise your student to do a few *mock interviews* (i.e., practice interviews) with a campus career counselor (or someone else) so that he can polish his interviewing skills.

Why

Interviewing, for most college students, is a weird and stressful experience—especially the first few times! Where else will your student feel such pressure to be "on" and to perform well in front of a bunch of strangers? That's why it's critical for your student to practice interviewing—in a setting where it's OK to make mistakes and then improve upon them. That's what *mock interviewing* is all about. Sadly, too few college students take advantage of mock interviewing—only to watch as their more interview-savvy peers land the best internships, co-ops, and jobs.

How

1. Encourage your student to contact the campus career center and set up an appointment with one of the counselors there. (Note: It's best if your

student can briefly talk to the counselor he'll be meeting with. He should tell the counselor that he'd like to do a mock interview, and then give the counselor some details about the type of internship/job he'd like to "interview" for, and with what "organization.")

2. A few days before the mock interview, your student should email his resumé to the counselor he'll be working with so that the counselor can effectively prepare for the discussion ahead of time. At the same time, your student should ask the counselor if it's possible for him/her to videotape (or at least audiotape) the mock interview. If it is, your student should tell the counselor he'd like to go ahead and do that. (This heads-up will allow the counselor to set up the appropriate equipment ahead of time.)

3. Encourage your student to prepare for the mock interview as best he can, knowing it won't go perfectly (not even close!). Remember: The idea at this point is not for your student to do everything right, but to *learn* how to do everything right!

4. On the day of the mock interview, your student should dress just as he would for the real thing. (That way the counselor can evaluate not only your student's interview performance but his attire and "look" as well.)

5. When your student arrives at the career center for his mock interview, the counselor will most likely go right into "interview" mode (just as the interviewer would do in a true interview). So your student should be prepared for the counselor to start playing his/her "employer" role right off the bat. Remember: The idea is for the counselor to simulate, as realistically as possible, the feel of an actual interview—complete with those somewhat awkward first few moments.

6. During the time your student is being "interviewed," he should stay in his role as the "job/internship seeker." He shouldn't slip in any asides to the counselor that he wouldn't say to an actual employer. Stress to your student the importance of making the mock interview as realistic as possible—which includes him being a little nervous!

7. Once the mock interview is done, your student will typically debrief with the counselor immediately. (If the interview was recorded, the two of them will watch or listen to it right away.) Usually, your student will

start by telling the counselor what *he* thinks he did well and not so well. Then he can ask the counselor for his/her critical feedback.

8. Suggest to your student that he write down the things he did well in the mock interview and, especially, the things he and the counselor feel he still needs to work on. Your student can practice these activities in additional mock interviews (a great idea!) or even, more informally, with family members and friends who are willing to help out.

9. Your student should be prepared to do more than one mock interview. (Most everyone needs at least two!) Much like riding a bike, interviewing gets easier with sheer practice. And that practice requires time and energy on your student's part. There are no shortcuts.

• ROAD MAP QUESTIONS TO ASK YOUR STUDENT •

Passions: Did your passion for your chosen career (or the company/ organization you were "interviewing" with) come across in your responses during the mock interview? How do you know?

Innate talents: Does interviewing come pretty easily and naturally to you, or is it a skill you'll have to work on? Do you need to practice telling people about your strengths and key accomplishments? Will you do yourself justice in your interviews for internships and jobs? How do you know?

What matters most: Do you know how to share your values appropriately? Are you able to explain why you'd be a good fit with a particular organization and *its* values? How do you know?

dreams ... discoveries ... reflections ...
intentions ... discussions

Mapping Your Direction

Uncovering Your Purpose
Sophomore Year

"The true profession of man is to find his way to himself."
~ HERMANN HESSE

Now that your student is in her sophomore year, her focus should be on examining her experiences and courses so far—and determining how she feels about what she's doing so that she can make some key decisions by the end of this year (such as what major to declare, for example, or whether she'd like to study abroad or pursue an internship).

This year, it's important for your student to truly connect to who she is and who she wants to become. Why? Because it's the best way for her to choose a meaningful, well-fitting academic major and, ultimately, a satisfying career. It's time for your student to find her own path—a winding one, no doubt (if she's like most people, at least!), but one she'll continue on for the rest of her life.

Your student will do this important work by exploring, examining, experiencing, and questioning everything that's important to her. She needs to awaken that part of her that is often hidden—sometimes by fear, sometimes by the many other voices in her life telling her to do something else. She needs to quiet those outside voices and listen to the most important one—the one within. This is the voice that will lead your student to finding her true purpose.

Purpose

The questions that follow will help your student begin to uncover his purpose. Help him take the time to thoughtfully ponder these questions—and the meaning of the answers that lie within him.

Are you living life your way? How so? What urges do you have that might be connected to your purpose? Have you started to connect to the things that hold meaning and purpose for you?

Dreams—Life's Destinations

This next set of questions is about your student's most inner desires. Your student may or may not want to share these with you right now. But encourage her to write down her responses—and when she feels like she wants to share them with you, be open to listening.

Do you have a deep inner desire to make sense of your life and the world around you? What are the opportunities you've experienced that have impacted you this past year? When have you felt totally fulfilled or inspired by something new—something that might become a part of your life dreams?

Discoveries

Encourage your student to think about important events and how he has felt connected through these events—something the following questions address. The things your student dismisses might be clues to greater meaning for him. So encourage him to answer these questions and, if he so chooses, to share his responses with you.

Scenic highways: How have you felt connected with your purpose this year? What has life been whispering to you? What do you feel deeply about or ponder every now and then that is truly important to you? (Examples: Perhaps you're thinking about living somewhere completely different, or becoming a specialist in a unique area of research because the learning itself moves you.)

_____

_____

_____

_____

_____

Roadblocks and speed bumps: What opportunities have you turned down because of fear or uncertainty? What do you want to do about it?

_____

_____

_____

_____

_____

Reflections

Reflecting helps your student turn her discoveries into action. It may take a lifetime for your student to understand her innate talents if she doesn't take the time to ponder them. So encourage her to write about what she really feels she does well. And make sure she knows this information can be totally private if she so chooses. Otherwise she may be too humble or fearful to write down what she really thinks.

Have you discovered your own wisdom? In the space below, take at least ten minutes to write freely about your innate talents—those abilities that come naturally to you. Alternatively, write freely about the things you've constantly been thinking about (i.e., what the world keeps whispering to you) but haven't yet acted upon.

Intentions

As a result of his activities, reflections, and discoveries, your student will have to take action to complete or even start something. That's where intentions and plans come in. So encourage your students to think about the following questions.

Set your course: Assess the meaningfulness in your life. Examine your relationships, the courses you're taking, and the activities you're involved in right now. How do these pieces of your life provide meaning for you? If they don't … what do you want to do about it? How will examining these aspects of your life help you move toward your dreams?

"People say that what we're all seeking is the meaning of life. …
I think that what we're really seeking is the experience of being alive."

~ Joseph Campbell

Daily intentions: Are you consciously choosing how you spend your time? How so? Do your decisions align with your purpose? Consider any nagging thoughts you have about what you "should" be doing each day. How can you act upon the thoughts that align with your purpose and eliminate the ones that don't?

Discussion and Dialogue

Discuss with your student the questions that follow.

Tap your support system: How have you become more aware of yourself, your talents, your interests, and what matters most to you in life? Ask someone from your support system to help you reflect upon these important questions. What does this person see as your strengths and innate talents? Do his/her observations seem congruent with how you see yourself? Does it matter?

_____

_____

_____

_____

_____

_____

_____

_____

_____

_____

_____

_____

_____

_____

_____

_____

Mapping Your Direction

Encourage your student to review his milestones and personal learning to plot his new direction with confidence.

How have your senses, thoughts, feelings, and intuition influenced your decisions this year? Do you have more clarity? What's still confusing to you? What do you need to do to get where you want to go?

_____

_____

_____

_____

_____

_____

_____

_____

_____

_____

_____

_____

_____

_____

_____

_____

_____

Junior
Year

• JUNIOR YEAR •

Experience

Introduction

Now it's time for your student to put what he's learned—about himself and the world of work—to the test! *Experience* is the focus of your student's junior year.

Experiencing a career or an industry is one of the best ways for your student to determine if that career/industry is a good fit for him. So while he'll be asked this year to continue some of the academic and experiential activities he's already been working on the last two years, he'll also be challenged to go a step or two further—and take what he's learned out into the real world.

This year, your student will focus on participating in wisely chosen internships, co-op opportunities, service-learning activities, and volunteer activities that will help him build specific skills. Perhaps, for example, your student has already been doing a bit of volunteering in college. What has he been *learning* through this activity? Can he continue to grow through this particular experience, or is it time for him to make a change?

The experiences of junior year are essential to your student's success in today's increasingly competitive entry-level job market. Whatever your student does at this point in his college career should challenge him and help him step out of his comfort zone—for only then will he fully develop the key skills and traits employers are looking for.

Your student will also need to start building his professional skills by learning how to network effectively, doing more *mock interviews* (i.e., practice interviews), attending job/career fairs, gathering letters of reference/recommendation, and perhaps even researching graduate or professional school entrance exams.

Your student may be tempted to put off some of these activities until senior year. Big mistake. Too often, college students lose opportunities during the first semester of senior year because they've failed to prepare for those opportunities ahead of time. For example, the job/career fairs your student will be attending senior year—so he can actually try to land a job—often happen in September or October. So your student needs to do some preparation before that—and junior year is the time to do it!

Parent/Student Road Map Activities

Experience Is Everything to Prospective Employers
In the eyes of future employers, your student's *experiences*—and the skills she gains from those experiences—are at least as important as the major she pursues in college. Getting experience during college is no longer merely optional for students; it's essential.

Internships, co-ops, volunteer activities, part-time jobs, studying abroad, joining campus organizations, job shadowing—all of these experiential activities will help your student:

- Explore career possibilities.
- Connect into "what matters most" to her—which in turn will give her a greater sense of purpose.

- Develop the skills and attitudes she'll need to land a job after graduation and remain engaged in lifelong learning

Listed below are seven questions you should discuss with your student to get her thinking about how and where she's gained valuable experience— or how and where she still *needs* to obtain experience:

1. Where have you been gaining "real life" experience?

2. Where can you obtain some (more) "real life" experience?

3. Do you currently have a part-time job? If so, what tasks do you do each day?

4. How can the tasks of your part-time job—and, especially, the skills you're developing in the process—transfer to a job in your future career area? Similarly, how can those skills transfer to "what matters most" to you in your future career?

5. What *soft skills* (e.g., written and verbal communication skills, problem-solving skills, critical thinking skills, analytical skills) have you been strengthening through your part-time job experiences?

• PARENT TIP •

Your student might well answer some of these questions with an "I don't know how ..." or "I can't ..." type of response. For example, she might believe that she cannot obtain a certain internship. Often this attitude stems from a fear of failure. So here's your chance to play motivator—and to question why your student has come to the conclusion she has reached.

6. Where have you volunteered and what skills have you gained from these experiences? What soft skills have you been strengthening through these experiences? What have you been learning about the world and your own values through volunteering? Where else could you volunteer?

7. What have you been involved with in your community? Where could you get involved in your community? How can you make a difference in your community—and help yourself feel more connected with the

community at the same time? How would these experiences help you explore careers as well?

Help your student break the situation down into pieces that the two of you can examine more closely. Perhaps, for example, your student believes she can't get the internship because of poor grades. If that is indeed true, you can help her create a plan for obtaining some other type of experience—something that *is* within her reach. The possibilities are practically endless, especially when you consider options like volunteering and service-learning.

Remember too, though, that often there are exceptions to the rule. So you might also want to encourage your student to see if the GPA requirement for her coveted internship is ironclad ... or not. Wouldn't it be a shame if she didn't even *apply* for the internship based on the *assumption* that her grades aren't good enough?

Help your student develop a plan to obtain (more) experience in the next six months—through an internship, a co-op, a part-time job, volunteering, community service, or some other activity. Remember: Future employers are expecting it!

Your Student's Career Path Will Be Winding, Not Straight

Turmoil, stops and starts, twists and turns—all will almost certainly characterize your student's future career path. Times have changed. Your student likely won't do any one thing for the rest of his professional life. So work with your student to reduce that common type of decision-making pressure by helping him think in terms of what to do *first* or *next* instead of what to do "for the rest of my life." Career decisions can be—and almost always are—changed at some point. They are flexible; nothing is permanent.

With that in mind ... think about how you can best support your student as he tries out possible careers during junior year. Talk to your student about your current job and your career path thus far. Use the age-old art of storytelling to take your student through your entire career to date, sharing with him the good, the bad, and the in-between. Your student wants—and needs—to hear about real-life situations.

Similarly, talk to your student about how the world has changed since you began your career. Technology has revolutionized the landscape of work,

• PARENT TIP •

Think back to when you were a teenager and you "knew" what you wanted to be when you grew up. Did you see yourself as a business person? a teacher? a graphic designer? a nurse? How well does that past vision match with what you're actually doing now?

Today your student has even more choices than you did, and technology is completely different than it was when you made your initial career choices. So in many ways, deciding on a career is even more confusing than it was in years and decades past—there's simply so much more to consider.

and jobs are created because of new discoveries every single day. Moreover, a business meeting no longer has to take place in one physical geographic location. Indeed, you can meet with people from all over the world—at the same time and in different time zones—thanks to technology.

Think of other examples to share with your student so that he realizes his career path won't be exactly like yours. More importantly, talk about how you've derived meaning from your work. What matters most to you in your day-to-day activities?

The Transferable Skills Your Student Needs

Helping your student understand her *transferable skills* is key to helping her secure future interviews and, ultimately, a future job.

In each of the transferable skills categories below, discuss with your student the directly related experience she already has in each area. Ask her to describe a specific instance of using that skill. If she needs more experience in a particular area, help her create a plan to obtain it.

A special note: The No. 1 transferable skill employers look for in college students/graduates is communication (written and verbal), so be sure to devote significant time to that particular category.

• COMMUNICATION SKILLS •

What employers expect	*Sample activities*
• Public speaking	Obtain job experience or volunteer
• Negotiation	
• Mediation	Interact with people of diverse backgrounds
• Listening	
• Multicultural sensitivity	Read to improve vocabulary and industry knowledge
• Nonverbal communication	
• Ability to convey messages clearly	Take a speech course
• Appropriate language usage (no slang)	
• Interviewing	
• Phone communication	
• Writing with correct grammar and usage	

What experiences have helped your student develop communication skills?

Experience 1
_____

Experience 2
_____

Experience 3
_____

• INTERPERSONAL SKILLS •

What employers expect	*Sample activities*
• Conflict management	Participate in team projects
• Stress management	Get involved in leadership activities
• Ability to give and receive feedback	Find a mentor for self-improvement
• Flexibility	Study abroad
• Teamwork	
• Leadership	
• Ability to work well with diverse groups	
• Sound business etiquette	
• Ability to motivate others	
• Adaptability	

What experiences have helped your student develop interpersonal skills?

Experience 1

_____

Experience 2

_____

Experience 3

_____

• M O T I V A T I O N •

What employers expect	*Sample activities*
• Initiative	Set goals and achieve them
• Confidence in abilities	Take on leadership roles
• Taking responsibility to get tasks done	Take pride in work
• Willingness to take risks	Engage in self-discovery
• Passion for work/career	Learn new interests
• Follow-through	Go above and beyond expectations
• Self-starting skills	
• Interest in continuing personal development	

What experiences have helped your student develop motivation?

Experience 1

_____

Experience 2

_____

Experience 3

_____

• ANALYTICAL SKILLS •

What employers expect	*Sample activities*
• Problem solving	Secure a business internship
• Ability to think outside the box	Take courses in statistics and logic
• Creative decision making	Conduct individual research
• Research	Reflect on how to solve problems
• Sound understanding of alternative views	Take a business finance course
• Ability to understand systems	
• Ability to understand businesses	
• Critical thinking and synthesizing	
• Ability to define needs	

What experiences have helped your student develop analytical skills?

Experience 1

_____

Experience 2

_____

Experience 3

_____

• ORGANIZATIONAL SKILLS •

What employers expect	*Sample activities*
• Solid time management	Build time management skills
• Ability to meet deadlines	
• Using an organizational system	Use a day planner/calendar
• Ability to delegate	Meet deadlines
• Ability to ask for help	Know what's expected of him/her
• Prioritization	
• Solid attention to detail	
• Evidence of multitasking ability	
• Ability to work independently	

What experiences have helped your student develop organizational skills?

Experience 1

_____

Experience 2

_____

Experience 3

_____

Adapted from Gradstaff, Inc.

Transferable Skills for Your Student's Career

Help your student create a list of the transferable skills she has developed through work or related experience:

_____

_____

_____

_____

_____

_____

_____

_____

Next, ask your student to list two jobs she would like to secure in the future. Have her list the key transferable skills that are likely necessary for success in each job.

Job 1:

_____

Job 2:

_____

How many of these skills does your student already have? _____

What can your student do to ensure she's building the transferable skills that will be essential to her in a future career?

_____

_____

_____

_____

Checking "The Voice Inside Your Head": Helping Your Student Stay Focused on the Positive

We often act one way on the outside but feel a whole lot different on the inside. Even college students who seem to have it all together may feel crippled or negative inside, where no one else sees it. Help your student assess the activity going on inside his head. The constant internal chatter he hears all day long ultimately influences what he does; thoughts become reality.

• PARENT TIP •

This is the year when your student will need to build confidence. As a junior, he will get to know his professors more deeply, pursue work related to his future career interests, and take on some leadership roles.

All of these activities require confidence. But your student may be feeling scared on the inside—and you may not know it. So don't be surprised if you see his mood swing back and forth from excited to almost depressed. It's entirely normal, especially if your student experiences a letdown of some sort. Support him by listening without judgment.

Part One

Ask your student to write down all the things he's thought about in the last thirty minutes and the internal "conversations" he's had. Do the same thing yourself.

We all live with this chatter every day. We need to acknowledge the thoughts and try to tune out the negative ones while capitalizing on the positive ones.

Part Two

Draw two columns on a piece of paper (and have your student do the same). Label one column "Negative/Pessimistic Thoughts" and the other "Positive/ Encouraging Thoughts."

Look at the running commentary you've both just written down. Record all of the thoughts that fit into the two categories.

Negative/Pessimistic Thoughts	Positive/Encouraging Thoughts

Part Three

Look at your lists of negative and positive thoughts. Start another list with the negative thoughts you need to acknowledge and let go, and encourage your student to do the same. Example:

Negative Thoughts to Acknowledge and Let Go
- I'm not smart enough
- I messed up on that quiz
- I'm not creative
- I'm fat

Now list a positive statement next to each negative statement—i.e., a thought to "turn on" for each thought you want to "turn off"—and encourage your student to do the same. Example:

"Turn Off" List	"Turn On" List
I'm not smart enough	*I'm really good at:*
I messed up on that quiz	*I'll study more next time or get a tutor*
I'm not creative	*I'm really great at analyzing data*
I'm fat	*I will make healthy eating choices today*

By changing his self-talk to focus on the positive rather than the negative, your student—with your help—will start feeling more confident, more balanced, and more hopeful about the future.

"Turn Off" List	"Turn On" List
_____	_____
_____	_____
_____	_____
_____	_____
_____	_____

*Adapted from "Changing Negative Thought Patterns into Positive Thought Patterns,"
Eileen Bailey, 2006*

Celebrate Successes

Celebrating small successes is a way for your student (and you!) to feel good about her continuing growth and development.

It's not easy for your student to find her career passions and prepare for employment in the four years or so it takes to graduate from college. Nor is it easy for you as a parent to act as a sideline coach through it all. So now is a good time to celebrate your student's successes large and small.

But you first have to define success and then plan for how you'll celebrate it.

Exercise

Think about what you're willing to do for celebrations/rewards for your student, as well as what would be good for your student to give herself. Be prepared to talk about the rewards you have in mind for various achievements. Remember: Rewards from others can be especially meaningful. Rewards can also take many different forms—from simply telling your student you're proud of her to having a special dinner for her or going on a trip in her honor.

With your student, think about her junior year and determine what tasks remain critical for her to complete in that time.

List those tasks here.

Critical task one:

_____

Critical task two:

_____

Now list the major goals your student needs to achieve by year's end.

Goal one:

_____

Goal two:

_____

Next to each critical task and goal, list a reward that would make your student feel great. Is it something you'll give or something she'll give herself?

Critical task one: Reward:

_____   _____

Goal one: Reward:

_____   _____

Finally, once your student has completed a few of these tasks and goals and you've celebrated those successes, ask her how it felt. Which rewards were most meaningful to her and why? Give her another opportunity to reflect on what's truly meaningful to her—and to deepen her learning about herself.

Academic Activities

- Encourage your student to continue striving for a high cumulative grade-point average (GPA)—at least 3.0 (on a 4.0 scale).

- Encourage your student to continue meeting with his academic advisor at least twice each semester.

• NEW TASKS •

Choosing Elective Courses

Encourage your student to use her elective credits to take courses (a) that complement her major, and (b) that are *seemingly* unrelated to her major—particularly in the areas of computer applications, foreign languages, communication (written and verbal), and research strategies.

Why

Remember the results of the National Association of Colleges and Employers' annual employer survey on *soft skills*? (If you don't, review this critical information on pp. 35-36.) Each year, written and verbal communication skills, analytical skills, and research skills are consistently cited as being among the top abilities employers look for when hiring new college graduates. Also consistently high on the list are computer/technical skills and foreign language capabilities.

The more of these skills your student can develop while she's in school—particularly through her coursework—the better positioned she'll be with prospective employers when she's trying to stand out from hundreds of other college students to land the job (or internship/co-op) she really wants.

How

1. Encourage your student to talk to other students she knows—especially other juniors and some seniors as well—about the elective courses

they've taken. What did those students like about their elective classes, and why? Could one or more of these courses be a good fit for your student's career-related wants/needs?

2. Encourage your student to skim through the *entire* list of courses available at her institution during the upcoming semester and see what titles jump out at her. Advise her to write down and research the courses that seem most intriguing. For example, she could email the professor who teaches the class she's interested in and ask about it. What will she learn? What is the professor's teaching style? How will this class enrich your student's life? (Note: This is also a good way for your student to test the professor. Is he/she courteous when your student contacts him/her? Does he/she give your student the time of day, or does he/she make your student feel like she's being a pest? If the latter is true, your student should think very carefully before signing up for a course from this professor.)

3. Advise your student to look closely at all the course options she has in the area of *communication*—the category employers always rank No. 1 on the list of soft skills they seek in new college graduates—and to take at least a few of her electives in this category. If possible, she should take an elective that taps into one of her strengths so that she can further develop that strength. Alternatively, your student can take a communication course that will help her develop a skill she hasn't had much experience with yet.

4. Encourage your student to ask her academic advisor for tips on what elective courses would strengthen the knowledge and skills she's gaining through her major courses—or that would nicely complement that knowledge and those skills.

5. If she can, your student should talk to one or more people who are working in the career she's thinking of pursuing after graduation. What elective courses do *they* recommend that your student take, and why? Are such courses available at the school? If so, your student can try to fit one or more of them into her schedule.

Passions: Is there a discipline you've always wanted to study but never had the chance to? Is there a discipline you know absolutely nothing about through which you could expand your career horizons a bit?

Innate talents: Is there a discipline you've never studied before that you might be good at if you were to give it a try? And are your computer skills, foreign language skills, communication skills, and research skills strong enough for you to be successful in the world of work? How do you know?

What matters most: Is there a discipline you've never studied before that might end up really mattering to you—in your career or in your life in general—if you were to simply give yourself a chance to understand what it's all about?

Getting to Know the Professors

Encourage your student to expand his efforts to get to know his professors. That way, by the end of this year, two or three professors will know your student well enough to speak highly of his academic (and perhaps out-of-class) achievements—in the form of a letter of reference, for example, or their willingness to recommend him to prospective employers (or graduate/professional school personnel).

Why

Professors who know your student well will be more motivated to write a good reference letter for him and help him in his future job search in other ways (e.g., introducing him to prospective employers, telling him about job openings they hear about). Indeed, professors who know your student well might be your student's first *networking* contacts, who can play a vital role in helping him get his career off to a great start.

How

1. Help your student pinpoint the classes in which he does well. Which ones intrigue him the most because of their subject matter? The profes-

sors of these courses are ones your student should get to know because he already has something in common with them—a shared passion for the discipline. Encourage your student to stop by during these professors' office hours and share a little about what he's hoping to do with his life. Your student can also ask for the professors' advice on how to get the most out of his courses and how to learn more about what those professors are teaching. Most professors enjoy helping students who are clearly and sincerely self-motivated.

2. Encourage your student to invite his favorite professor out for coffee on campus to learn more about how that professor found his/her career. (Note: Some colleges/universities have special funds set aside that students and/or professors can use to pay for these coffee sessions [or even lunches or dinners together!] because they want to actively encourage out-of-class interactions between students and professors. Does your student's school have this type of program? Has your student checked?)

3. Once your student has begun developing a good relationship with a particular professor, encourage him to keep that professor in the loop when, for example, he's applying for internships or jobs. Your student should ask this professor—ahead of time—if he/she would serve as a reference to prospective employers (or graduate/professional schools).

4. Remind your student to sincerely acknowledge his professor by sending a brief email or card of thanks for anything that professor does for him. Not only is this simple act a form of common (but too often overlooked) courtesy; it's also a way of ensuring that the professor will *continue* offering his/her help to your student in the future. (After all ... when you thank someone for his/her efforts, he/she is more likely to continue putting forth such efforts.)

• ROAD MAP QUESTIONS TO ASK YOUR STUDENT •

Passions: Is there a professor you know who is so passionate about his/her discipline that you can't help but become passionate about it yourself? Who is that professor, and what is it about his/her subject area that intrigues you so?

Innate talents: Have you gotten to know at least one professor who can speak intelligently and accurately about your abilities and skills—in a letter of recommendation, for example, or in discussions with prospective employers or graduate/professional schools?

What matters most: Is there a professor who has gotten to know you well enough to understand what really makes you tick—that is, what you value (in life and in work) and how you want to carry out what you value in your day-to-day activities? Does this professor understand what really drives you? If so, how might this professor help you (a) envision a future career, and (b) grab the attention of prospective employers or graduate/professional schools?

Research Courses and Independent Study Seminars

Encourage your student to take a research course or an independent study seminar that allows her to complete a major research project (i.e., a "thesis") on a topic of very strong interest to her.

Why

Developing solid writing skills is essential no matter which career path your student ultimately pursues. In fact, in the annual *soft skills* survey conducted by the National Association of Colleges and Employers (see pp. 35-36), employers consistently cite communication (written and verbal) as the *No. 1* soft skill they look for in college students and recent college graduates. By researching and writing a major paper, or *thesis*, your student will be able to not merely *say* she has strong writing skills, but *prove* it.

Still, that's not the only reason your student should complete a complex research project during her time as an undergraduate. Doing so will also:

- Give her hands-on experience in conducting research as well as studying the research findings of others. Employers consistently rate research skills as high on the list of soft skills they seek in college students and recent grads.

- Allow her to develop some expertise on a topic she enjoys studying—a topic that may well be part of her career someday. What better way for your student to shine in a job interview than to be able to quote the findings of her own research on a specific issue or problem in her chosen field?

- Help your student develop a solid connection with, for example, a professor who advises her on her research project, or with an off-campus professional (e.g., the internship supervisor who allows her to conduct a survey of all the interns in the company) who helps her carry out that project.

How

1. If your student's institution or academic department *requires* the completion of an intensive research project/thesis, encourage her to sign up to begin on that task starting this year.

2. Most academic departments offer an Independent Study (or similarly named) course each semester, through which your student can complete a research project for an agreed-upon number of credits. Encourage your student to look for these courses in various departments of interest. Perhaps she can arrange an Independent Study in collaboration with a professor in one of those departments.

3. Encourage your student to ask a few of her professors about any research needs within their departments. (Example: The psychology department would like to know why so many students do poorly in its "Abnormal Psychology" course.) Perhaps your students could be an essential part of uncovering some answers!

4. Some schools have an Undergraduate Research Opportunities Program (UROP) designed for undergraduates who want to complete major research activities. This type of initiative is another option your student can explore. (Note: She may even be paid for her work through a program of this type.)

5. Encourage your student to approach a student affairs professional on campus and ask him/her if the student affairs division could use any research help. Perhaps, for instance, the school is seeing too many students leave after freshman year and wants to know what's going on. Your student's research project could help the school find out.

6. Encourage your student to take an hour sometime to sit in a quiet place and think about the many "why" questions she likely has now that she's in her junior year of college. Possible examples: "Why do colleges and universities spend so much money on athletics?" "Why are so many

political advertisements so negative?" "Why do the heads of major companies so often commit criminal offenses related to company finances?" What does your student naturally wonder about in her life? Perhaps one of these topics—if she can focus it a bit with the help of a faculty advisor—would make for an excellent major research project.

• ROAD MAP QUESTIONS TO ASK YOUR STUDENT •

Passions: Which disciplines and topics interest you so much that you want to learn about them in great depth? What do you find yourself reading about (or watching on TV or listening to on the radio) just for its own sake (i.e., not because you have to for a class)?

Innate talents: Can you handle the difficult tasks involved in developing, executing, and writing up the results of a major research project? Do you have conceptualization skills? research and interviewing skills? written and verbal communication skills? Additionally, do you have a natural curiosity about a certain topic? If so, do you have enough drive to devote significant time and energy to studying it?

What matters most: What problems and issues in life truly need addressing, in your opinion? What, in your view, are the needs of the world and the big questions that need to be answered? What topics do you feel so strongly about that you find it impossible to ignore them or brush them aside?

Career Development Courses

Suggest that your student take a course on career development or the job search process, and that he work hard to do well in it—not just for the grade but for his personal benefit as well.

Why

By taking a career development or job search course, your student can work on many of the same tasks he's completing throughout *The College to Career Road Map*—but in a more formal way, and under the guidance of a career development expert. The course will also force your student to meet certain deadlines for various activities—a good bonus if he tends to otherwise put things off, no matter how helpful they might be to him. (It's one thing to say, "I'll put together a resumé ... sometime"; it's quite another to say, "I need to have my resumé done for class by the end of the day on Friday.")

How

1. Encourage your student to see if his academic department or school/college offers a career development course for students in his major or school/college. If it does, he should register for the course as soon as he can.

2. If your student's academic department or school/college does *not* offer a career development course, your student can contact the campus career center and see if *it* offers a career development course (for credit). If it does, he should register for the course as soon as he can.

3. If your student can't find a for-credit career development course anywhere at his school, he can see if the campus career center offers shorter, non-credit seminars or mini-courses on career development and job search tactics. If it does, your student should attend one or more of these seminars or mini-courses as soon as he can.

4. Encourage your student to consider taking a career development or job search course via online/distance education—either through his own institution or another.

5. Your student should also consider taking a career development or job search course through his institution's college/school of Continuing Education—or through the Continuing Education department of another nearby college or university. (Your student doesn't necessarily have to take a career course at *his* institution to gain the knowledge he needs.)

6. Another possibility your student should consider: taking a career development or job search course at an institution near where he lives during the summer months.

Passions: Is your career development/job search course helping you gauge what your strongest interests are? Conversely, is it giving you a good idea of what you *don't* enjoy (which can be as critical as knowing what you *do* enjoy!)? What fields/industries intrigue you at this point? How do you know? Have you gained this knowledge from a career assessment like the Strong Interest Inventory? from an experiential activity like an informational interview? from a book or web site you read to learn about a certain career area?

Innate talents: Is your career development/job search course helping you better understand what you're naturally good at (i.e., your innate talents)? Is it helping you pinpoint the skills you've learned over the years through various educational and work experiences? Which of your abilities and skills are the most fun for you to use? the least fun? (Remember: It's one thing to be *good at* something; it's quite another to *enjoy* that something!)

What matters most: Is your career development/job search course helping you gain a better sense of what really matters to you in life—especially in your future career? Are you learning, for example, where you stand in relation to key work-related values like job security, salary, and power? How about other key values like independence, creativity, and decision making? What will you *refuse to tolerate* in your future career? Conversely, what will make you jump out of bed each morning excited to go to work?

Experiential Activities

- Encourage your student to continue collecting items for her *career portfolio*, and to have her portfolio done by at least mid-year (see tips for doing so in this section, p. 154) so she can use it in on- and off-campus interviews with employers.

- Encourage your student to continue researching careers in more depth by not only reading about them, but also talking (in person or via phone/email) to people who actually work in them (i.e., *informational interviewing*).

- Encourage your student to continue researching companies and organizations she might want to work for someday.

• NEW TASKS •

Seeking a Leadership Role in a Campus Organization

Encourage your student to take on a high(er)-level leadership role in at least one campus organization.

Why

If your student got into a lower-level leadership position in a campus organization during his sophomore year, wonderful! Now it's time for him to continue his growth by pursuing a higher-level position—such as being an officer (e.g., treasurer, vice president, president) in the organization.

Why? Several reasons:

- Employers who hire new college graduates consistently report that they're looking for grads who have hands-on *leadership* skills and experience. (Revisit the results of the *soft skills* survey of employers conducted annually by the National Association of Colleges and Employers—see pp. 35-36). Leading a student group is a natural way for your student to get that experience and develop sound leadership abilities for the future.

- As a high-level leader of a campus organization, your student will get to know—on a personal basis—several key faculty members on campus (among them his group's faculty advisor); key members of the student affairs staff on campus; and, on occasion, local professionals/employers in the group's area of focus. The people in all three of these broad groups might someday provide solid references for your student. As importantly, they'll likely pass along internship and/or job leads to your student. (After all, if they see your student in action as a strong leader on campus, why *wouldn't* they make him aware of ways to do the same thing off campus?)

- As a high-level leader in a campus organization, your student will almost certainly be compelled to learn (or polish) skills in essential areas like budgeting and financial management, recruiting, marketing and public relations, team building, communication (written and verbal), and fundraising. Expertise in just one of these areas (let alone several) will, by itself, make your student stand out in relation to most other college students and recent graduates. (If your student were an employer, wouldn't he be more likely to hire someone who *has* these skills and experiences vs. someone who *does not* have them?)

How

1. Your student should look critically at the campus organizations he's involved in and identify where more (or better) leadership is needed. If no leadership position exists to address those areas, your student can volunteer to take on that role alone. Conversely, if addressing those areas requires your student to be in a high-level leadership position within the organization, encourage him to put his name in for consideration.

2. As your student considers high-level leadership positions that are filled by new people each school year, encourage him to examine his own strengths and interests. Will he be most effective—and will he have a more rewarding experience—if he's the president of the group? Or is he a better fit for a different high-level position, such as treasurer, vice president, secretary, fundraising chairperson, or recruiting chairperson?

3. Encourage your student to also talk to people who hold (or have held) high-level leadership positions in his student group. What do these people like about their jobs? What do they dislike? Where do they see your student fitting in best when it comes to a high-level leadership role? Might one of them serve as a sort of mentor to your student as he seeks to land a high-level leadership position in the organization?

Passions: Do you enjoy leading a group from a big-picture standpoint—i.e., as a high-level officer in a group, who worries less about day-to-day details and more about the overall direction of the organization? Or do you prefer leading at a lower, more grassroots level where you have a chance to get your hands dirty? How might this knowledge affect you in, say, your first job after you graduate from college?

Innate talents: Are you a born leader? If so, how do you know? If not, are you starting to learn sound leadership skills? How do you know?

What matters most: Is it important for you to take a strong leadership role in the activities/issues that matter to you, or would you prefer to be a strong follower or colleague instead? Do you want (need?) to run the zoo, or are you content with simply working at the zoo? (Or is the truth somewhere in between—i.e., do you prefer a mid-level leadership role?)

Revising the Resumé

Encourage your student to revise her resumé to reflect the experiences, skills, and accomplishments she gained during sophomore year and the summer following sophomore year.

Why

By this time in your student's academic career, her resumé is probably going to look vastly different from the first draft she developed freshman year. That's good—because as she's already come to know (hopefully!), a resumé is a living document that needs to change as she changes and grows. Indeed, it would be foolish for your student to continue using the same resumé she wrote freshman year. After all, she'll almost certainly have more experiences, skills, and accomplishments to brag about now vs. a couple of years ago. How will an employer ever know about those achievements if your student doesn't revise her resumé?

How

1. Encourage your student to make an appointment with a campus career counselor to revise her resumé.

2. Before the appointment with her career counselor, your student should take three sheets of paper and—just as she did last year for this same purpose—label them "New Experiences," "New Skills," and "New Accomplishments," respectively.

3. Encourage your student to use the "New Experiences" sheet to jot down any new experiences she can think of that have occurred between her sophomore year and now. It's critical that your student *not limit herself at this point!* If something jumps into her mind—no matter how minor or insignificant it might seem—she should write it down! The idea is to do a "brain dump" and get everything out of her head and onto paper. Later, she can decide, with her counselor's help, what to add to her resumé and what to leave off.

4. Encourage your student to go through the same "brain dump" exercise with the "New Skills" and "New Accomplishments" sheets.

5. Once your student has finished writing down everything she can think of on each of these sheets, she should keep them in a handy spot…just in case she thinks of other entries to add later.

6. Encourage your student to bring all three of these sheets to her appointment with the career counselor. That way, she can ask the counselor for help remembering anything she may have forgotten or disregarded.

7. With the counselor's help, your student will decide which entries to add to her resumé and which to leave off. As was the case last year, she'll almost certainly have to do some reformatting of her resumé to accommodate the changes—that's par for the course.

8. Once your student has finished revising her resumé, she can ask her career counselor to look at it one last time for minor revisions.

• ROAD MAP QUESTIONS TO ASK YOUR STUDENT •

Passions: Does your revised resumé reflect what you're passionate about—especially any new topics/issues/concerns you've become passionate about in the last year or so? How do you know?

Innate talents: Does your revised resumé highlight the new skills and experiences you've gained over the last year or so? Are they easy for the reader to quickly spot? How do you know? Have you been specific about these achievements, and have you quantified them wherever possible (e.g., "Increased group membership by 20%")?

What matters most: Does your revised resumé clearly illustrate what you represent and what matters most to you? Is it easy for the reader to quickly spot this essential information? If the reader had just ten seconds to look at your resumé (not an unrealistic possibility, by the way!), would he/she be able to get a basic sense of who you are and what you're about? Are you sure?

• FACT •

"Upper management is raising the performance bar at all levels, and hiring managers want to interview and hire only candidates who specifically have the skill sets, talents, and motivations that match the job qualifications. They're almost shouting, 'Show me the proof you have exactly what I'm looking for!'"

~ RICK NELLES, NATIONAL DIRECTOR OF COLLEGE RECRUITING FOR THE PRINCETON SEARCH GROUP AND AUTHOR OF *PROOF OF PERFORMANCE: HOW TO BUILD A CAREER PORTFOLIO TO LAND A GREAT NEW JOB*

The Career Portfolio

Encourage your student to get started on creating a *career portfolio* highlighting his accomplishments and skills.

Why

Every day, employers interview job applicants who *tell* those employers about their skills and experiences— "I can do this," "I can do that." The frequent problem (from the employer's perspective) in this scenario: Applicants can (and often do) say *anything* in interviews to put themselves in a good light, sometimes stretching the truth and—more often than you'd like to think—telling outright lies to employers.

That's why most employers today are looking for *evidence* that your student can do what he *says* he can do, and that he's really done what he *says* he's done. He can provide that evidence—and then some—by developing a *career portfolio* and using it in his job and internship interviews.

A career portfolio is simply a professional-looking, three-ring binder in which your student can display tangible evidence of his past accomplishments and current skills. For example, it's one thing for your student to mention on his resumé an award he's won; but he'll make more of an impact on a prospective employer if he can show that employer a picture of himself receiving the award, as well as the actual award itself. All of that can be on display in your student's career portfolio.

What your student includes in his portfolio is limited only by his imagination. He might display excellent papers he's written, publications he's developed, honors he's received, photos of activities he's been involved in, letters of recommendation or congratulations he's received, highlights of interesting class projects he's completed, and much more. In doing so, he will be among the few job applicants who can *show* an employer what he has to offer—not just *talk about it*.

There's a more intangible (but no less important) benefit too, especially if your student anticipates job interviews being nerve-wracking experiences: If your student has a portfolio on hand, he'll have a "prop" of sorts that he can use to more effectively tell the employer about himself and his achievements. He can use his portfolio to do a mini show-and-tell of his skills and accomplishments—which is generally much easier than recalling everything from memory and then trying to recite it to the employer.

In short, your student just can't go wrong by developing and using a career portfolio. On the contrary, a portfolio will boost his confidence and improve his job interview performance.

How

1. Your student will need to go to the campus bookstore or a nearby office supply store and buy a *nice* three-ring binder. (This isn't the time for your student to be frugal and buy a binder of the $2.99 variety. Encourage him to spend $20 instead to get a good binder that will look professional—and that will last.)

2. Additionally, your student will need to buy some section dividers for the binder, along with some clear plastic display pages (with hole

punches on the side) and some labeling tabs (with labels). He'll use all of these materials to create various sections for his portfolio, and to then label those sections and fill each one with the clear plastic pages (where his actual materials will be displayed).

3. Next, your student will need to find the box in which he's been saving his future career portfolio materials the last couple of years (see p. 42). (Note: If he hasn't been saving materials in a special place, urge him to start gathering materials together now. He can put them in a box or some other container where they'll all be in one place.)

4. Encourage your student to look through the materials he has and sort them into four or five basic categories. Some possibilities: "Academics," "Student Activities," "Volunteer Activities," "Awards/Honors," "Work/Internships," "Leadership Experience," "Communication Skills." There is no one "right" way to do this! Your student just needs to make his best attempt to organize the materials in a way that will make sense to someone else who looks at his portfolio (i.e., a prospective employer).

5. Once your student has finished developing his basic organizational scheme, he can use the labeling tabs and section dividers he bought to create the main sections of his portfolio. Within each of these sections, he can put in a few clear plastic display pages.

6. Now your student can go ahead and put his materials into the plastic display pages, each in the appropriate section.

7. If he wants to, your student can use a word processing program to create brief captions for each of his portfolio items. Example: "Receiving the Outstanding Leader award from University of Arizona President Judy Jones, April 30, 2006." (Note: Not only will these captions help the person who is reading your student's portfolio; they'll also help your student as he talks about the various items during his interviews.)

8. If your student gets stuck during any part of the portfolio development process, encourage him to get some help from a campus career counselor, his academic advisor, or other students he knows who have created portfolios themselves. Alternatively, he can consult one of several useful books on career portfolios:

- *The Career Portfolio Workbook*, by Frank Satterthwaite and Gary D'Orsi (published by McGraw-Hill, 2002)

- *Creating Your Career Portfolio: At a Glance Guide for Students*, by Anna Graf Williams and Karen J. Hall (published by Prentice Hall, 2004)

- *Proof of Performance: How to Build a Career Portfolio to Land a Great New Job*, by Rick Nelles (published by Impact Publications, 2000)

• ROAD MAP QUESTIONS TO ASK YOUR STUDENT •

Passions: As you look through your completed (for now!) career portfolio, do you get the sense that someone reading through it (i.e., a prospective employer) will be able to see evidence of what your strongest interests and passions are? If not, what materials can you add to your portfolio to make your passions/interests stand out more effectively?

Innate talents: Will someone reading through your portfolio (i.e., a prospective employer) see some proof of your key abilities and skills? Have you considered showing your portfolio to someone who doesn't know you very well and asking him/her to tell you what abilities and skills he/she sees evidence of in your portfolio?

What matters most: Will someone reading through your portfolio (i.e., a prospective employer) get a good idea of what's most important to you—especially in your work and career-related activities? How do you know?

Networking

Help your student begin *networking*—starting with people she already knows and then moving to people she doesn't know (yet!)—so she can build relationships with people in various organizations and industries.

Why

Networking is, by far, the best way for your student to learn about careers and organizations. After all, who better to tell your student about a career or company than someone who is actually working *in* that career or company? As importantly, networking is the most efficient and effective way for your student to find a job when she graduates—or even an internship or a co-op while she's still in school. If she puts herself in the shoes of an employer, it's easy to understand why.

Imagine your student is an employer and she needs to hire someone for a job or an internship. More than likely, her own job is on the line—in some ways, at least—because she needs to make a good hiring decision. (If she doesn't, her bad hire will cost the organization money in the form of wasted salary, wasted time, and wasted effort—and her own supervisor will thus be displeased.) Moreover, if your student-turned-employer is like many professionals, she's already been burned at least once by a job candidate who made lots of great-sounding claims in the interview, but didn't live up to any of them on the job.

So your student-turned-employer is naturally cautious. She's a bit skeptical. And she certainly isn't going to hire just anyone for this job. What can she do to minimize her risks? One of two things:

- Interview and hire someone she already knows very well—someone she can trust because this person has proven himself/herself trustworthy in the past.

- Interview and hire someone who comes highly recommended by someone she knows and trusts—after all, if someone she trusts can vouch for this person, the candidate must be a good risk.

Now your student can begin to see why networking—starting now—is so critical to her job or internship search(es) later. By networking now, she becomes a known quantity to prospective employers. And employers will always hire a known quantity over an unknown quantity. It's faster, it's easier, it's almost always cheaper, and—most crucial of all—it's decidedly less risky.

How

1. Your student should start her networking efforts by first talking to people in her own life instead of total strangers. She'll be surprised at the expertise and connections that are right in her own circle of acquaintances. For example, she could talk to neighbors, parents of her college or high school friends, former teachers, and even people you or her other relatives know. She can ask all of these people about their careers

and their places of employment. Do they know about any internships or jobs that might be a good fit for your student? Are they willing to simply keep their eyes open and contact your student if they hear about any such internships or jobs? (Note: More than likely, they *are* willing; but they won't know to contact your student unless and until she asks!)

2. If your student prefers communicating in writing versus in person, she can network by emailing people who are in careers/industries of interest and asking them questions. Or she could use email to introduce herself and then invite the person she's contacted out for a face-to-face conversation over coffee.

3. One of the easiest and most effective—but too often overlooked or discounted—ways your student can network is to join and get involved in a professional organization in her field of interest. In many cases, professional organizations have campus chapters and/or local chapters your student can join—typically for a very low cost. If she then simply starts attending the regular meetings of the campus and/or local chapter, she'll start getting to know people in her field—and giving them a chance to get to know her.

4. Whenever your student talks to a networking contact, encourage her to focus on asking for just two things: information and advice. Your student doesn't want to fall into the trap of making people feel like she's simply hitting them up for a job. So instead, encourage her to ask only for *information* and *advice*—both of which anyone can readily and easily provide. Your student will still get the feedback she needs; but she'll do so in a way that doesn't make her networking contacts want to turn and run away!

5. Your student should also consider developing a one-page *leave-behind paper* highlighting her key interests/passions, abilities and skills, personality traits, and career goals. She can then carry copies of this document with her—instead of or in addition to her resumé—each time she meets with a new networking contact face to face. If your student gives a copy of her leave-behind paper to all the people she talks to, they'll remember her weeks or months from now—and perhaps pass her information on to other contacts.

6. Every time your student talks with a new networking contact, remind her to ask the person if he/she knows of other people your student should talk to—and if he/she will help your student connect with these other people by, for example, making an introductory phone call or sending an introductory email on her behalf. At a minimum, your student should ask each new networking contact if she can "namedrop" his/her name to the next person she tries to contact. For example: "I spoke with Jane Smith the other day, and she suggested I contact you." It's always a little easier for your student to find a new networking contact when she can say she was referred by someone that person already knows.

7. After each chat she has with a new networking contact, your student should send or email that person a quick thank-you note. It's common courtesy, for starters. But it will also help your student stand out in that person's mind as a conscientious, professional person who is worthy of being helped.

• ROAD MAP QUESTIONS TO ASK YOUR STUDENT •

Passions: As you talk to various people through your networking efforts, which of them are engaged in day-to-day activities that really grab your interest? What are these activities that you find so inherently fascinating, and why do you like them so much?

Innate talents: How are your "people" skills? Can you make people feel comfortable talking with you, and are you comfortable talking with them? If not, how can you improve this essential skill? Additionally, are the people you're networking with giving you a better sense of where you might best put your favorite talents and skills to good use? Do you see any patterns in the feedback you're getting?

What matters most: Among the people you network with, who seems really satisfied with their work, and why? Are there any people who seem unhappy with their work? What seems to make them so dissatisfied? Do you see any patterns?

Utilizing Mock Interviews

Urge your student to do some additional *mock interviews* with a campus career counselor so that he can hone his presentation skills in preparation for real job or internship interviews.

Why

When (if?) your student participated in *mock interviews* (i.e., practice interviews) during his sophomore year (see p. 108), he no doubt discovered how valuable they are in helping him get ready for real interviews. Well, this year he's going to start *having* real interviews—for internships and/or jobs—so practicing some more, ahead of time, will help him prepare to do his very best.

Remember: Employers will be expecting your student to do a solid job of presenting his skills, education, and experiences in an interview situation. Employers will want your student to carry himself well and back up his statements with solid evidence. Sound stressful for your student? It is! That's why practicing with a career counselor—and discussing his performance immediately afterward—is so critical to his future success in interviews.

How

1. Encourage your student to set up a mock interview appointment with a campus career counselor. If possible, your student should arrange for the mock interview to be videotaped (or at least audiotaped) so that he can watch (or listen to) himself afterward and critique his performance with the help of the counselor.

2. Remind your student to get his resumé into the career counselor's hands a few days before the mock interview so that the counselor can prepare for the discussion in advance.

3. Your student will want to choose a specific job at a specific company to "interview" for and let his career counselor know, ahead of time, what that job and company will be. That way, the counselor can develop specific questions that align closely with the questions your student will potentially be asked during a real interview with that company.

4. To the degree possible, your student will need to prepare for the mock interview just as he'd prepare for a real interview. At a minimum, he

should research the organization and jot down some questions he can ask during the discussion.

5. On the day of the mock interview, your student should dress just as he would for the real thing. (That way the counselor can evaluate not only your student's interview performance but also his attire and "look" as well.)

6. Once the mock interview is done, your student should debrief with the counselor immediately. He can start by telling the counselor what *he* thinks he did well and not so well. He can then ask the counselor for his/her insights. The feedback he receives after a mock interview is the most important reason for doing a mock interview in the first place! So urge your student not to just interview and run.

• ROAD MAP QUESTIONS TO ASK YOUR STUDENT •

Passions: When you start having real interviews, will you be able to truly demonstrate your interest in (a) your chosen field, (b) the organization you're interviewing with, and (c) the job at hand? How will you prove your interest to often skeptical employers—most of whom have been burned at least once by interviewees who claimed things in an interview but didn't live up to those claims on the job?

Innate talents: Are you prepared to effectively describe your abilities and skills in response to the various types of questions employers will likely ask you—*general* (e.g., "Tell me about yourself"), *situational* (e.g., "What would you do if ____?"), and *behavioral* (e.g., "Tell me about a time in the past when you had to _____.")? How do you know?

What matters most: Can you effectively tell prospective employers what's important to you in your work, in the organization you work *for*, and in the people you work *with*? How do you know?

Professional Organizations Related to Career Choice

Encourage your student to join and get involved in at least one professional organization related to her chosen major and/or career.

Why

College students who are involved in professional organizations tend to impress the professional members of those organizations. By being in a professional organization during college, your student will demonstrate that she's committed to her field of interest.

Encourage your student to put herself in the shoes of a prospective employer. Scenario: She's interviewing a couple of new college graduates for an entry-level newspaper reporting job. One of the candidates has been an active student member of the local Society of Professional Journalists (SPJ) chapter for the last two years. (Your student-turned-employer knows this for a fact because she's seen the candidate at many of the SPJ meetings.) The other candidate has no involvement with SPJ.

Which of these new-grad candidates, in the eyes of your student-turned-employer, is likely more committed to and focused on newspaper journalism as a career? The evidence strongly suggests it's the first candidate—thanks in no small part to that candidate's involvement in a professional organization.

How

1. If your student is involved in a campus organization, she should see if it has a connection with an outside professional organization—at the local level, the state level, or even the national level. If it does, she should visit the web site of this larger, outside professional group and see how she can join and get involved.

2. Encourage your student to ask professors and her fellow students about professional organizations they're aware of that might be a good fit for her. She can then visit the web sites of the suggested groups and see if any of them will be of professional benefit to her.

3. Encourage your student to use an Internet search tool like Google (www.google.com) or Yahoo! (www.yahoo.com) to search for professional associations in her field(s) of interest.

4. Encourage your student to go to the campus or local public library and ask a reference librarian there to show her the print or online version of the *Encyclopedia of Associations* (or a similar resource) so she can search for professional organizations by topic area or geographic area.

5. Once your student finds a professional organization to join, urge her to do so—and to start attending its regular meetings at the local level, if possible. (Your student can find announcements of those meetings on the organization's web site—or, in many cases, in the business section of her local daily newspaper.) It's one thing for your student to simply receive a professional group's publications or use its web site resources; but she'll benefit even more by getting to know some of the actual people in the organization face to face—and helping them get to know her.

• ROAD MAP QUESTIONS TO ASK YOUR STUDENT •

Passions: What are the people in your new professional organization doing in their careers that excites you? What about the organization's publications grabs your interest? How about its conferences?

Innate talents: As you interact with people in your new professional organization and read its publications, what are you learning about the key abilities and skills that seem to be critical in this field?

What matters most: What seems to matter most to the people in your new professional organization? How well do these values match up with your own—especially where your future career is concerned?

Job/Career Fairs

Encourage your student to familiarize himself with the job/career fair environment by attending at least one job/career fair, on or off campus.

Why

It won't be long until your student embarks on an extensive search for a full-time job. One of the many ways he can do just that is to attend a job/career fair, where prospective employers come together in one place—

usually a large auditorium of some sort, either on campus or off—to recruit prospective employees.

Making the most of a job/career fair is part science, part art. Your student needs to learn how to effectively approach the employers in attendance, introduce himself, and—perhaps most difficult of all—talk about himself and the education, skills, and experiences he has to offer. It can be exciting, yes; but it can also be intimidating and nerve-wracking, at least in the beginning.

Encourage your student to simply plan on attending a job/career fair during this, his junior, year so that he can observe a bit. That way he can get used to the feel of the atmosphere and eavesdrop on a few conversations between other students and employers. Which students seem to be doing the best, and what exactly are they doing to make themselves stand out? By observing, your student can find out. And he can also pinpoint what the employers in attendance seem to be asking about or looking for consistently.

Encourage your student to jot down some notes on what he sees and hears so he'll have something to refer back to next time he attends a job/career fair—when he'll probably really be competing with the rest of the attendees to land a job.

How

1. Early in your student's junior year, encourage him to stop by the campus career center or visit its web site to get a sense of what on- and off-campus job/career fairs will be offered in the school's geographic area in the coming months. (Note: Sometimes your student will have to sign up in advance if he wants to attend a particular fair—so urge him to follow any requirements that have been set out by the career center and/or the sponsoring organization[s] of the fair.)

2. Remind your student to keep an eye on the career section of the local newspaper (or its web site). Often, local job/career fairs are sponsored by—or at least publicized by—newspapers as a service to readers.

3. Encourage your student to stop by any local government or nonprofit agencies that focus on career issues (e.g., a local workforce center, a nonprofit career counseling agency)—or visit their web sites—to keep abreast of upcoming job/career fairs in the area.

4. Once your student chooses a job/career fair to attend, encourage him to prepare a few copies of his resumé to bring with him … just in case he runs into employers who would like a copy (or to whom he'd like to give a copy!).

5. Help your student dress appropriately for the fairs he attends. Usually, *business casual* dress—somewhere between shorts-and-flip-flops and suit-and-tie—is appropriate. If your student is in doubt, he's far better off being *over*dressed versus *under*dressed!

6. When your student arrives at the job/career fair, he'll need to check in at the registration table, pick up any materials that are being handed out, and put on a name tag if one is offered to him. Then it's time for him to start walking around the job/career fair, listening and observing and getting a feel for the event. How are people acting and interacting?

7. Encourage your student to look for employer tables/areas that are surrounded by lots of attendees. He can then go over by the other attendees to observe and listen if he'd like, yet blend in at the same time. By using this "eavesdropping" strategy, your student will give himself a chance to learn vicariously—through the words and actions of others.

8. If he wants to, your student can talk to an employer or two before he leaves the job/career fair. If your student sees an employer he's really interested in, he should stop and talk to a different, less-interesting employer first. That way he can practice under less pressure before approaching the employer he's really interested in!

9. If/when your student talks to an employer, he should be sure to ask for the employer's card before he goes—and to leave a copy of his resumé with that employer too.

10. Within twenty-four hours after the job/career fair is over, your student should send or email a thank-you note to the employers he spoke with at the fair. Your student will stand out for this simple but too-often-ignored act of gratitude.

• ROAD MAP QUESTIONS TO ASK YOUR STUDENT •

Passions: During your time at the job/career fair and in your reflection shortly thereafter, what specific companies/organizations really got you pumped up? Why? Which companies/organizations offer products, services, or causes that truly excite you? What's so interesting about these products/services/causes?

Innate talents: When you were at the job/career fair, did you come upon any companies/organizations that could potentially tap some of your best (and favorite) abilities and skills? What sorts of things could you do for this organization? Where might its needs match up with your talents? How could you someday market your key abilities and skills to this organization?

What matters most: At the job/career fair, did you learn about any companies/organizations whose products, services, or causes might be a good fit with what's most important to you in life? Moreover, did you find out about any organizations where your career would bring you the rewards *you* want—be it a high salary, job security, work/life balance, great co-workers, or whatever?

Researching Graduate/Professional Programs

If applicable to her situation and goals, your student should start research-ing graduate/professional programs and preparing to take required entrance exams (e.g., GRE, GMAT, LSAT, MCAT).

Why

Your student will need to start the research process now if she plans to attend graduate or professional school. Why? So she doesn't miss any crit-ical deadlines.

Your student should also decide if she wants/needs to attend graduate/professional school right after she finishes her undergraduate degree or instead work for a year or two and then attend. Some graduate/professional school programs—particularly MBA (Master of Business Administration) programs—prefer or even require that students get some real-world experience to be considered for admission.

How

1. Encourage your student to set up an appointment with a campus career counselor, and to let that counselor know that she wants to research graduate/professional schools and learn more about the process of applying to them.

2. Your student should then go to the campus or local bookstore and page through some of the many books available on graduate/professional school and how to get in. (Note: These books are published by companies like Peterson's and Princeton Review.) Your student can also visit web sites like Peterson's (www.petersons.com) and Princeton Review (www.princetonreview.com) to find additional information on graduate/professional school and how to get into the program of her choice.

3. Each graduate/professional school program your student comes across will have information on its minimum admission requirements (GPA, entrance exam scores, courses taken) as well as the program's averages for GPA and entrance exam scores. Encourage your student to look for this information; it will give her a good idea of how well a particular program might fit her (or not).

4. Preparation programs for graduate school entrance exams are widely available—sometimes right on campus but more typically off campus via private companies and self-study programs (e.g., books, computer software, videos). Help your student assess whether she has the discipline to prepare for her graduate/professional school exams on her own. Will the structure and expertise offered by a preparation program be worth the cost where *your* student is concerned? Why or why not?

5. Encourage your student to ask her professors and other trusted adults in her life if it would be better for her to go to graduate/professional school right away or to instead get some real-world experience first. Urge your student to talk to people who have a wide variety of perspectives!

Passions: What graduate/professional programs interest you the most? What can you see yourself studying for the next two to five years or more? Why?

Innate talents: In which graduate/professional programs are you most likely to be successful from an academic standpoint? Additionally, will you be able to do well enough on any graduate/professional school entrance exams you'll need to take? How do you know? Might you need to invest in a test-preparation program of some sort, on or off campus? Why or why not?

What matters most: What graduate/professional programs will help you prepare for the life you want to live after graduation (whatever that may entail!)? How do you know?

Skill-Building Experiences

The Value of Internships

Support your student in completing at least one internship or co-op experience during his junior year (or the summer immediately following junior year).

Why

Given today's increasingly competitive entry-level job market, doing an internship or co-op is no longer *optional* for college students; in employers' minds, it's *essential* experience for college students to obtain while they're in school.

Just how important is internship or co-op experience? Consider these eye-opening research findings.

• FACT •

Employers offer full-time, permanent jobs to 58 percent of the students who do internships with their organizations and 60 percent of the students who do co-ops with their organizations, according to the 2004 Experi- *ential Education Survey conducted by the National Association of Colleges and Employers (a trade association for college/university career services professionals and employers who hire new college graduates).*

Why these high numbers of interns-turned-employees? Because these students have already proven themselves to their respective employers—and employers will hire proven experience over unproven lack of experience every single time.

Your student simply must—*must*—get some experience through an internship or a co-op before he graduates. If he doesn't, he'll struggle to keep up with the thousands of other college students and recent grads who *do* have internship/co-op experience.

How

1. If your student has been tracking internship/co-op possibilities in an "Internship/Co-op Possibilities" binder since his sophomore year (see p. 103), great! Now is the time for him to return to that binder and make some decisions about which opportunities he'd like to pursue.

2. If, on the other hand, your student is just beginning to research internship or co-op possibilities, he can:

   • Visit the campus career center (or its web site) and check out the internship and co-op listings it has obtained from various organizations.

- Check out a college-oriented career web site like MonsterTRAK (www.monstertrak.com), Experience (www.experience.com), CollegeGrad (www.collegegrad.com), or CollegeRecruiter (www.college recruiter.com) and look for internship and co-op listings there.

- Go to the campus library or a nearby bookstore and look through one of the many printed internship directories that are on the market (published by companies like Princeton Review and Peterson's). (Note: At the bookstore, your student will find such guides in the "Careers" or "College Guides" section.)

- Talk to his professors and fellow students and ask them where current and previous students from his school/department have done internships or co-ops in the past. (Note: Employers often prefer hiring new interns or co-op students from the same schools/departments where they've had success doing so in the past. Urge your student to take advantage of this phenomenon!)

- Talk to a counselor at his school's career center (particularly if the center has an *internship coordinator* or similarly titled person on staff). Your student can ask the counselor/coordinator where previous students from the school have interned or done co-ops in the past.

- Directly approach any organizations that interest him and ask (by phone or email) whether they have internship or co-op opportunities for college students.

3. Once your student has decided which internships/co-ops he'd like to pursue, encourage him to use his current resumé and an accompanying cover letter to apply for those internships/co-ops. (Note: If your student needs help with either his resumé or his cover letter, encourage him to *get it*—preferably from a counselor at the campus career center. There's absolutely no reason for your student to try to create/revise these key documents completely on his own, especially when expertise is available—for free—at the campus career center!)

4. If/when your student gets an interview for an internship/co-op, advise him to prepare for it thoroughly by working with a campus career counselor to research the organization, practice responding to interview questions (in a *mock interview*—see p. 161), and develop a list of questions he'd like to ask during the interview.

5. If/when your student lands an internship or a co-op opportunity, he needs to show the organization he's an outstanding hire by:

- Listening well and asking questions from the get-go.
- Showing up on time and looking professional every day.
- Completing his assigned tasks before deadline.
- Demonstrating his willingness to take on the "grunt" work along with the more-challenging assignments.

As you undoubtedly know from your own experiences, your student is being evaluated from Day One of his internship/co-op—not just on his technical skills but also on his people skills (e.g., attitude, teamwork, self-motivation). If he makes a good impression, there's a decent chance he'll eventually be offered a full-time, permanent job with this organization!

• ROAD MAP QUESTIONS TO ASK YOUR STUDENT •

Passions: Do you enjoy working in your internship/co-op setting? Why or why not? Is your internship/co-op exposing you to *new* interests—ones you didn't know you had before?

Innate talents: Are you good at what you do in your internship? How do you know? Do you have the *hard* skills as well as the *soft* skills (e.g., working well with others, making sound decisions, being self-motivated) you need? If not, how could you develop them?

What matters most: Now that you've seen this setting/career/industry firsthand, does it seem like it will allow you to live the life you want to live after graduation (whatever that may entail!)? If not, what's missing?

The Importance of Volunteer Activities

Encourage your student to participate in additional volunteer activities (see p. 37) to further strengthen the key *soft* skills (e.g., communication, teamwork, leadership, initiative) future employers will demand—and to show prospective employers that she actively cares about the world around her.

Why

Some core skills are critical to your student's professional success no matter which field/industry she eventually pursues. Each year, the National Association of Colleges and Employers (an industry trade association for college/university career services professionals and employers who hire new college graduates) asks its employer members which *soft* skills are most important for college students and recent graduates to have. Consistently in the top ten (see pp. 35-36) are communication skills (written and verbal), teamwork, leadership, and initiative (self-motivation).

Your student not only needs to *have* these essential skills by the time she graduates; she also needs to be able to *prove* it to prospective employers. As was the case when she did it during her first two years of college, volunteering will allow her to do just that.

But volunteering is more than simply a way for your student to develop professionally. Indeed, it goes far beyond *her*. By volunteering, your student shows future employers (and the rest of the people in her life) that the many needs of the world matter to her, and that she's willing to do something about them in a tangible way. If your student was an employer, wouldn't *she* be impressed by an entry-level job candidate who clearly and actively does something about problems he/she sees—without expecting anything in return? That's what volunteering is all about.

How

1. Encourage your student to see if her school has an office devoted to matching students with local volunteer opportunities. (Note: The office will probably be called something like Volunteer Opportunities or the Service-Learning office—or it may be a department of a larger organization like Student Activities.) If it does, urge your student to visit the office and learn how she can volunteer in a way that matches her interests and skills and fits her schedule.

2. If your student is involved in a campus organization, encourage her to see if it coordinates any volunteer activities in the area. If it does, your student can participate. If it doesn't, perhaps your student could be the person to launch such an effort. (Talk about developing her leadership skills!)

3. Encourage your student to see if her academic courses include a required *service-learning* component. If they do, she's got a built-in volunteer/service experience set up already. If not, encourage her to schedule a course—next semester!—that does have a service-learning component.

4. If your student goes to school in a fairly large city, urge her to contact the local chapter of the United Way. Often, the United Way serves as a local clearinghouse of volunteer opportunities. Alternatively, your student can use the United Way web site (www.unitedway.org) to search for volunteer opportunities in her area, or use another web-based search tool like VolunteerMatch (www.volunteermatch.org).

5. Once your student finds a volunteer opportunity to pursue, encourage her to keep a journal of her activities. What sorts of things is she doing when she volunteers? What is she learning? She should write it all down now … so she doesn't forget it later!

• ROAD MAP QUESTIONS TO ASK YOUR STUDENT •

Passions: What's most interesting about your volunteer activities? Are there any activities you *don't* like? What are they, and why don't you like them?

Innate talents: What new skills are you learning through your volunteer activities? What skills are you developing further? Which of your volunteer activities come ridiculously easy to you? Which ones are quite difficult?

What matters most: Which of your volunteer activities are naturally motivating to you? Why do these activities inspire you so strongly? Conversely, which activities feel forced or uninspiring to you? Why?

dreams ... discoveries ... reflections ...
intentions ... discussions

Mapping Your Direction

Uncovering Your Purpose
Junior Year

"To accomplish great things, we must not only act
but dream, not only plan but also believe."

~ ANATOLE FRANCE

This is the year when your student will need to choose his experiences wisely and perhaps take a few calculated risks as well. It will be in his hands to go after his dreams and grab the experiences that fit him best.

Purpose

The questions that follow will prompt your student to really think about what he's looking forward to and how that fits his direction or purpose in life. Your student will need to begin understanding what really gets him "jazzed" in the way of a vocation.

What has been revealed to you in the activities you've pursued this past year? When have you felt really satisfied in the past few months? Why? What are you now looking forward to, and why does this vision excite you so much?

Dreams—Life's Destinations

Dreaming and creating steps to reach his dreams are a big part of your student's junior year. He needs to examine how each of his experiences feels and whether it was in line with his dreams. The following questions will help your student uncover some of this information.

Now that you've been exposed to a variety of work and volunteer activities, your natural inclinations will provide a sort of direction through the ebb and flow of your interests. Some of your activities this past year—work, volunteering, service—have no doubt prompted feelings of heightened interest. Which activities did that for you? How do these connections relate to your dreams? Where do you want to go at this point in your life?

Discoveries

The questions that follow will help your student focus on what she really loved about her experiences this year and weave them into a purposeful work fabric for her future.

Scenic highways: How connected have you felt to your purpose this year through your various activities—working or interning, volunteering, participating in a student or professional organization? What's become clearer to you with respect to the kind of work you truly love?

Your student also needs to consider the things that caused her to pause this year. The questions below will help.

Roadblocks and speed bumps: As you think about your experiences this past year, which ones just didn't resonate with you? Which of them felt awkward ... or just didn't fit your style ... or didn't hold any interest or meaning for you? How might these insights impact your decisions about the work you want to do in life? And what career-related activities would you like to do that you haven't had the time and/or energy for (yet!)?

Reflections

Your student needs to leave college knowing that he's on a new adventure, and that it's up to him to harvest the goodness from his relationships to develop more goodness in the many new relationships he will be encountering in his work (and elsewhere). Good relationships make life enjoyable. If your student understands what he can offer and what he needs in a relationship, he will feel a sense of community rather than a sense of loneliness in his new life. The next set of questions will ask him to ponder his relationships.

Have you discovered your own wisdom? Set aside some time when you can be completely alone. Find a quiet place where you can do some reflection. Think about your conduct in relation to other people in your life, and consider what you've received from and given to these various relationships. What are you grateful for and what do you feel best about? What's important to you in your relationships as you ponder your future career decisions?

In the book *The Myth of Maturity* (W.W. Norton & Company, 2001), author Terri Apter notes that a constant source of disappointment among recent college graduates is the often less-than-satisfying quality of their various workplace relationships. Knowing what a satisfying relationship is for *you* will be critical to you in the coming months as you finish college and head for the world of work.

Intentions

Help your student understand her intentions by advising her to address the questions that follow. It's easy to put off those things in life that we don't have a plan for. So encourage your student to look at what she really wants and to then create a plan of intentions around it. What skills does she still need to develop further to reach her dreams?

Set your course: What skills or special knowledge do you want to develop this year through your various activities and experiences? What will you commit to that will move you toward gaining this knowledge? What have you observed about your own thoughts and feelings this year as they relate to your work and volunteer experiences? What have you noticed that you want to capitalize on or change?

_____

_____

_____

_____

Daily intentions: How well are you developing relationships in your work settings? Are you satisfied with them? What's important to you in a work relationship? What can you do each time you go to work to make your relationships there more fulfilling?

_____

_____

_____

_____

_____

Discussion and Dialogue

Encourage your student to have in-depth discussions with all types of people in his work and volunteer settings. He could even ask someone to be a mentor in his career area so he can get some professional guidance. The following questions will help.

Tapping your support system: What do you want to accomplish this year in your work or internship/co-op experiences? Talk to people in your work/internship/co-op setting and let them know what you'd like to achieve. Then ask each of them if they'd be willing to guide you as you pursue these goals.

Mapping Your Direction

The entire *College to Career Road Map* is about making *decisions with direction*. So encourage your student to assess how everything is going and feeling at this point. That way she can decide whether she wants to continue on in her current direction or make a slight change in course. The questions that follow will help.

How have your senses, thoughts, feelings, and intuition influenced your decisions this year? Do you have more clarity? What's still confusing to you? How would you evaluate your self-confidence at this point? When it comes to your future career, what do you need to do now to get where you want to be later?

Senior Year

Employment and Education

Introduction

Your student's senior year will probably be the most challenging of her college career. Indeed, there will be times this year when she'll feel overwhelmed because she'll need to:

- Pay attention to her academics so she keeps her grades up.
- Continue picking up solid experience through a job, an internship, or a co-op.
- Take on a leadership role in a campus organization or another group.

She'll also have to focus on the future—her life after graduation. So she'll feel like she's living in two worlds at times: college and post-college. But there's good news too: Over the last three years, your student has pursued opportunities and wrestled with questions that have likely helped her start seeing the future with a bit more clarity.

(Note: If she hasn't, encourage her to go back through her college memories now and start thinking about the experiences that have been most meaningful to her. Now is the time for her to ask herself why. The questions throughout this book are designed to help your student better understand her future—her passions, her innate talents, and what matters most to her. It's never too late for her to work through these questions!)

The phases of Exploration, Examination, and Experience are behind your student. Now, it's time for her to look to her post-graduation future. Whether that means employment or graduate/professional school in her particular case, uncovering her purpose is key to her success and satisfaction!

Parent/Student Road Map Activities

Presentation Is as Critical as Preparation

Your student can be incredibly prepared for the world of work, academically and even experientially; but if he can't effectively present himself— in person and on paper—he won't get as far as he would like. So encourage him to develop a *career portfolio* featuring evidence of his key abilities, skills, and accomplishments.

To land a post-graduation job, your student will also need to create a top-notch resumé and cover letter. Moreover, he will need to effectively share stories about his experiences so that he can prove to prospective employers what he has to offer over competing candidates for the job.

Helpful resources are available to your student right on campus—at the school's career center. So be sure to encourage him to tap the many services offered there. In the meantime, you can help your student become an effective presenter during the job search by completing the following activities with him.

Portfolio Creation/Refinement

If your student hasn't already created a *career portfolio* (see p. 154), encourage her to develop one now. She should buy a high-quality, three-ring binder and some clear page inserts from an office supply store. She can then gather any awards, special acknowledgments, work references, photos, and documents that will serve as evidence of her key experiences and skills.

The career center at your student's school can then show her how to effectively use a career portfolio in interviews, as well as what the finished portfolio should look like. Your student can also consult one or more of the following helpful books on career portfolios:

- *The Career Portfolio Workbook*, by Frank Satterthwaite and Gary D'Orsi (published by McGraw-Hill, 2002)

- *Creating Your Career Portfolio: At a Glance Guide for Students*, by Anna Graf Williams and Karen J. Hall (published by Prentice Hall, 2004)

- *Proof of Performance: How to Build a Career Portfolio to Land a Great New Job*, by Rick Nelles (published by Impact Publications, 2000)

Resumé Review

Now is the time for you and your student to critically evaluate his resumé. Specifically, it needs to do an exceptional job of illustrating his education, experiences, and skills in relation to the type of job he will be pursuing after graduation.

Review the previous sections of *The College to Career Road Map* (see pps. 44, 99, and 152) to see what your student should have already done for his resumé. Then encourage him to go to his school's career center so that an expert there can thoroughly review his resumé to ensure it's not just average, but outstanding. Anything less will hurt his chances in the highly competitive entry-level job market.

Skill Stories

Many employers now use a technique called *behavioral interviewing* (sometimes called *behavior-based interviewing*) when they're evaluating candidates for jobs. Behavioral interviewing features questions that ask for specific examples of what the job candidate has done in the past to develop certain key skills or traits.

For example, suppose a prospective employer concludes that the ability to work well on a team is an essential competency for the job the employer is trying to fill. When the employer brings in your student for an interview, then, he/she will almost certainly ask a "behavioral" interview question focusing on your student's ability to work with other people. The question might look something like this:

*Tell me about a time in the last year when you had to work well
with a group of other people to complete a certain task or project.*

Your student will then be expected to offer an actual example of her team-work skills. Responding with "I *would* do _____" or "I *think I could* do _____" won't cut it. She will have to go beyond the hypothetical. So strongly encourage her to practice telling stories from her past experiences using the STAR (**S**ituation/**T**ask—**A**ction—**R**esult) method outlined in the upcoming "Focus on the Future" section (see pps. 212-214). Be sure your student has, at a minimum, stories offering evidence of her abilities in key *soft skills* like communication (written and verbal), problem solving, leadership, and self-motivation.

You should also encourage your student to visit her school's career center to obtain a list of questions that are often asked in recent-graduate job interviews. Encourage your student to complete a few *mock interviews* (see p. 108) as well, with a campus career counselor or another experienced professional.

Networking

Help your student understand what networking is (and is not!). Then encourage him to start networking, beginning with baby steps. Here's how the two of you can work together on this key task:

• PARENT TIP •

*Some of the jobs that might
fit your student well are never
advertised. So it's imperative for
him to understand the importance
of networking—and to learn
how to network well. Don't be
surprised, however, if your student
is a little less than excited where
networking is concerned. It's not
an easy activity for most people.
So be patient.*

1. Help your student look at his list of potential networking contacts. Encourage him to choose a few of the people from this list and contact them—via phone or email/letter—to ask for career advice and ideas … nothing more. If he can arrange brief conversations with a few of the people on the list, so much the better.

• PARENT TIP •

Don't let your student fall into the "I don't know anyone!" or "I don't have a network!" trap. We all know some people. Encourage your student to begin his networking activities with people he already feels comfortable with and to then branch out from there. For example, even though Uncle Fred doesn't work in the field your student is interested in, he might well know someone else who does.

2. Tell your student about any of *your* personal contacts who might be of help to him in his career activities. Offer to make the initial contact with these people to see if they'd be willing to chat with your student. Then turn things over to your student and encourage him to set up the actual appointments. It's fine for you to open doors where your own contacts are concerned; but your student has to walk through those doors alone, particularly if he wants to have any credibility with working professionals.

3. Tell your student about networking events that are coming up in your geographic area in the coming months. Encourage him to monitor the events calendar on campus as well. For example, many campus organizations host various activities that can be great networking opportunities for your student.

4. Help your student prepare a *leave-behind paper* (see p. 159) for use during his networking activities. This document—which your student can leave with the people he talks to—might include information about his strongest interests, abilities and skills, and values as well as a brief summary of what he feels he will contribute to an organization.

5. Help your student create a system to track his networking contacts (i.e., whom he has spoken to about what, and when). And be sure to empha-

size to your student the importance of sending thank-you notes to each and every person who has been helpful in his career activities.

A Tracking System for the Job Search Process

Sit down with your student and discuss how she is going to track the resumés and cover letters she sends out, as well as the responses she receives. Encourage her to develop a computerized tracking system using Microsoft Excel or even a simple Microsoft Word document.

Your student should also track her follow-up activities—like checking to see if an application has been received or sending out thank-you notes.

No Need to Go It Alone

Career work—especially in today's complex world—is difficult. It can make your student's head swim, to say the least. Fortunately, help is available all around him in the form of career counselors and coaches (particularly at the campus career center), mentors, teachers, friends and family members, and, of course, you.

Encourage your student to tap into the career expertise that's available to him. There's absolutely no need for him to go it alone where career activities are concerned. So make sure he knows that just because he's graduating doesn't mean he has to make every decision single-handedly and become an instant adult. Let your student know you'll continue to be supportive, and that he can always turn to you in times of need.

This is critical reassurance for your student to hear—from you. Today's world is often overwhelming and frightening, and it will be even more so to your student if he thinks you now expect him to work alone. He still needs your guidance and unconditional love. He will face

• P A R E N T   T I P •

Don't assume your student doesn't need you anymore—even if he acts like it. (Sound like the teenage years?!) It's more than likely a cover—his way of acting like he thinks you want him to act.

plenty of bumps on the road in the years to come. He will be able to better navigate those obstacles if he knows you're always there—not to do things *for* him but to help him if he needs it.

Conversation One

Help your student think of three people she knows who she can always count on for support after graduation. How can your student reach out to these people?

Conversation Two
(The Most Important Conversation)

Talk with your student about how you plan to be there to support him through the entire transition from college to the world of work. Reiterate that your parenting activities don't simply stop at graduation.

Your student will no doubt express tremendous relief during this conversation. Why? Because the world tells him the opposite—that he is flying solo once the graduation ceremony is over. Years ago, that was probably true. But today's world is different, and it will likely take your student longer to start acting (and feeling!) completely like a mature adult.

How will you be a solid support system for your student through this critical transition period? Let him know!

Academic Activities

• CONTINUING TASKS •

- Encourage your student to continue striving for a GPA of at least 3.0 (on a 4.0 scale).

- Encourage your student to continue meeting with her academic advisor at least twice each semester—particularly to ensure she's taking the courses she's supposed to be taking to complete her degree.

- If your student plans to study abroad during senior year (see p. 31), encourage her to make sure she's still meeting all of the academic requirements to graduate on time. She should get prior approval for all of her study-abroad courses so that she's not surprised—unpleasantly—when she returns to campus expecting to graduate.

- Encourage your student to continue taking skills-based courses with her remaining electives—ones that complement her major and ones that are seemingly unrelated to her major. She should focus in particular on the areas of computer applications, foreign languages, communication (written and verbal), and research strategies.

- If she hasn't done so already, encourage your student to take a research course or an independent study that allows her to complete a major research project (i.e., a *thesis*) on a topic of strong interest (see p. 145).

• NEW TASKS •

Writing Courses

Encourage your student to strengthen his writing skills by taking an additional writing course or by working on the writing he's doing in other courses.

Why

Depending on the coursework he's taken to this point, your student may or may not have had someone critically evaluate his writing outside of his first-year composition course. The papers he's written have certainly been graded for content, but ideally your student should have been required to rewrite his papers at least once to improve his skills.

Strong writing skills separate your student from his peers. Remember: Communication (written and verbal) is the No. 1 *soft skill* employers seek in new college graduates, according to annual surveys of employers conducted by the National Association of Colleges and Employers (see p. 35-36).

How

1. Encourage your student to take an additional upper-level writing course that will help him focus specifically on improving his writing (and rewriting and editing!) skills.

2. If your student's school has a Writing Center (or a similarly named office), urge him to use it! The staff members there will review your student's writing and offer helpful feedback on how he can make it better.

3. Help your student embrace the process of rewriting papers. College is demanding, and sometimes just getting a paper written is the best your student can do. But if he works toward finishing his papers a week early, he'll build in time for other people to critique his writing. Indeed, he can give his papers to several people—the professor teaching his class, for instance, or a teaching assistant or a Writing Center advisor or even a friend who has exceptional writing skills.

• ROAD MAP QUESTIONS TO ASK YOUR STUDENT •

Passions: Do you enjoy writing? Do you spend extra time on writing assignments just to get the language right?

Innate talents: Are you a strong writer? Are you able to effectively convey your ideas in writing? Does writing come easily to you?

What matters most: Do you value improving your communication skills—especially when it comes to writing? Are you willing to spend extra time on this area if you need to? If so, what will you do to improve your skills?

The Application for Graduation

Encourage your student to complete her application for graduation by the deadline established by her institution.

Why

Your student does want to graduate ... doesn't she? Seriously, though, just talk to one student who has missed the application deadline for graduation (and who thus didn't officially graduate until the following semester) and you'll quickly understand how important it is for your student to take care of this essential task sooner vs. later.

How

1. Have your student check with her academic advisor or the Registrar's Office at her school to see *exactly* what she needs to do (and by when) to officially apply for graduation from the institution.

2. Once your student has the paperwork she needs to apply for graduation, urge her to complete it immediately. She can procrastinate on other tasks in her life if she must, but she doesn't want to put this one off! You don't want your student to run into any hitches that would prevent her from graduating on time—and with her close friends.

3. Once your student has submitted her completed application for graduation, she should *insist* on getting some sort of receipt acknowledging that her application was received and approved. (She'll need this receipt later if the institution somehow claims she never applied for graduation. Yes, it happens ... more often than you might think, unfortunately.)

• ROAD MAP QUESTIONS TO ASK YOUR STUDENT •

Passions: Are you excited to start putting your knowledge, skills, and experiences to work in the real world? Why or why not?

Innate talents: Do you put off little details like applying for graduation, or is it in your nature to get things done right away, without procrastination?

What matters most: Is it important to you to graduate on time, or are you dreading leaving college? Are you spending time planning carefully for the future, or are you living in the moment?

Seeking Professional References

Encourage your student to decide which of his professors can be the best spokesperson for him, and to then ask that professor if he/she is willing to be a professional *reference* (either for a post-graduation job or for graduate/professional school).

Why

At some point this year, your student is going to start applying for post-graduation jobs (or graduate/professional schools, as the case may be). As part of that process, he's going to need some strong *references* who will speak highly of his skills and abilities, his performance, and his commitment to his chosen field.

If your student is like most college students, at least one of his best references will come from a professor he's gotten to know very well (and who in turn has gotten to know him very well). If your student can get great references from not just one professor but two or three, he'll be even more impressive to prospective employers (or graduate/professional school admissions personnel).

How

1. Encourage your student to contact a few of his favorite professors and ask to meet with them. Your student should prepare for these meetings just as he would for other *networking* opportunities. He should be ready to ask each professor for what he needs: solid references! Your student should bring along to each meeting his resumé, his *leave-behind paper* (see pps. 159 and 191) if he has one, and, if applicable, any graduate/professional school application forms the professors might need.

2. Remind your student that he's probably not the only student asking for a reference from a particular professor. So he should give the professor all the information he/she might need to do a good job on a reference letter. Ideally, the completed reference letter will be specific and detailed, giving the reader the sense that the writer genuinely knows your student and has accurately and thoroughly assessed his abilities, interests, and motivations.

3. If your student doesn't know any of his professors well enough to ask them for a professional reference, it's not too late. Encourage your stu-

dent to choose a course he's enjoying now and to take a moment imme-diately after an upcoming class session to talk to the professor before he/she leaves the room. Your student should tell the professor that he's finding the course topics genuinely interesting, and that he'd like to learn more about them outside of class. If your student can spend the next few months cultivating a relationship with the professor, that pro-fessor just might become a valuable reference for your student before his college days are over.

• ROAD MAP QUESTIONS TO ASK YOUR STUDENT •

Passions: Do you feel comfortable sharing what you're passionate about with your professors so that they in turn can act as knowledgeable references for you? Can you communicate your passions clearly, succinctly, and credibly?

Innate talents: Do you have at least one professor who will, for example, write a letter of recommendation for you (for jobs or for graduate/professional school) attesting to your skills and abilities in your chosen discipline (or another)?

What matters most: Is there at least one professor who has gotten to know you well enough to understand what truly matters to you in your future career?

Experiential Activities

On-Campus Interviewing
Encourage your student to participate in on-campus interviewing through the campus career center to become acquainted with various companies/organizations—and, potentially, to land a post-graduation job.

Why
Many employers already have ongoing relationships with career center staff at various colleges/universities—in great part so they can recruit stu-dents from those institutions for jobs, internships, and co-op programs.

One of the most common recruiting tools these employers use is *on-campus interviewing*. It's one of the rare instances in the world of work when employers are willing to go find—literally and figuratively—prospective job candidates. So your student would be foolish not to take advantage of it.

Typically, campus career centers bring employers to campus in the fall and again in the spring. One of those employers might well be looking for *your student*. Will she be found? If she participates in on-campus interviewing, she'll certainly improve her odds!

How

1. Encourage your student to contact or stop by the campus career center—or to visit its web site—to see when on-campus recruiting will begin in the fall (or in the spring, as the case may be).

2. Remind your student to complete any registration requirements the career center has in place for participation in on-campus interviewing. (Note: Your student will typically have to submit a version of her resumé along with a cover letter. She might also have to complete some demographic information forms.)

3. Advise your student to prepare for on-campus interviews just as she would any other job interview (see pps. 108-110). She should research the organizations she's pursuing, dress professionally, and practice responding to questions she think she'll be asked. These are *real interviews* for *real jobs*. So your student shouldn't try to wing it!

4. Urge your student to talk to a campus career counselor about the organizations she'll be interviewing with during on-campus recruiting. Campus career counselors almost always have strong working relationships with the employers who come to campus. Your student can tap that expertise.

• ROAD MAP QUESTIONS TO ASK YOUR STUDENT •

Passions: Are you prepared to share what you're passionate about with the prospective employers who participate in your campus career center's on-campus interviewing program?

Innate talents: Are you prepared to effectively describe your abilities and skills to prospective employers? Do you have stories and examples to back up each of your claims? Are those stories and examples compelling?

What matters most: Are you ready to put interviewing at the top of your priority list? And will you be able to communicate to prospective employers what matters most to you in your career and in the organization you'll ultimately work for?

Job-Search Workshops

Encourage your student to attend one or more brief job-search workshops offered by the campus career center.

Why

There's no sense in your student tackling his post-graduation job search all alone when help is readily available right on campus—in the form of the counselors at the campus career center.

Most career centers offer a variety of short (a few hours or less) seminars on job-search strategies. Urge your student to take advantage of these workshops. He'll learn about everything from writing effective resumés and researching organizations to preparing for interviews and negotiating job offers.

How

1. Encourage your student to stop by the campus career center—or to visit its web site—to learn about the job-search seminars it offers. Your student should sign up for the workshop he needs the most and then gauge how helpful it ends up being for him. If he has a good experience, he can sign up for other workshops in the weeks and months to come.

2. Urge your student to actively participate in the workshops he attends so that he gets the most he can from each experience.

3. If your student has any nagging questions or concerns after a particular workshop, encourage him to discuss them with the instructor—either immediately following the workshop or in a one-on-one career counseling appointment a few days later. Your student shouldn't let his questions go unasked (or unanswered)!

Passions: How are your deepest passions starting to show themselves in the workshops you're attending at the campus career center?

Innate talents: How will you effectively describe your innate talents on a resumé, in an interview, or during the networking process? What tips are you picking up from the career center workshops you're attending?

What matters most: Are the workshops you're attending helping you clarify what matters most to you in your future career? Why or why not? What types of questions do you have about your work-related values, and how can you start getting some answers to them?

The Job Search Support Group

Encourage your student to get a few of her friends together and create a job search support group.

Why

Friends can be among your student's best resources—and sources of support—during this sometimes difficult phase of her life. In some ways, your student's friends might know her better than she knows herself. So they can often help your student process the many decisions she'll be faced with during the job search process.

Sometimes, conversations with friends are the "aha" moments your student will never forget—for example, the night she really figured out what she wants to do with her life. Friends can also point out your student's strengths, her innate talents, and her strongest values—all of which factor greatly into her career future. So talk to your student about inviting her friends to participate in an informal job search support group. They can all help each other help themselves.

How

1. Encourage your student to ask her friends if they're stressing out over the post-graduation job search—like she is. Your student will likely be surprised at the widespread level of anxiety among her fellow students.

Indeed, they may feel relieved that someone else has acknowledged needing support and has taken the lead in making it happen.

2. Encourage your student to meet with the members of her informal support group at least every other week so that they can all update each other on their progress (or lack thereof). The group members should hold each other accountable for the tasks they really need to accomplish.

3. If your student and her fellow group members want to attend on- and off-campus job/career fairs together, fine. But remind her that the students in the group shouldn't talk to prospective employers as a team or a pack. They can check in with each other from time to time to share experiences and tips.

• ROAD MAP QUESTIONS TO ASK YOUR STUDENT •

Passions: What do your friends think you're passionate about? Are they right? Do they see—even if you cannot—how you can use your passions in a future career?

Innate talents: What do your friends see as your innate talents? Do you agree? Why or why not?

What matters most: When you ask your friends to identify your top values, do they list the values you see as your most cherished ones? If not, is it possible that your actions sometimes conflict with what really matters to you, especially in a future career?

Evaluating Campus Organization Experience

Help your student evaluate what he's done in the campus organizations he's in and prioritize what he still needs to do during his senior year.

Why

It's one thing for your student to merely participate in a campus organization. But employers who hire new college graduates consistently report that they're looking for grads with leadership skills and experience.

Employers demand specific examples of what your student has accomplished in college. Leading a student group is a great way for him to add to his list of accomplishments and develop sound leadership skills. So now is the time for your student to figure out what accomplishments and skills he's already taken care of and, perhaps more importantly, which ones he still needs to take care of during this last year of participating in a student group.

How

1. Encourage your student to take a couple of sheets of paper and label them "What I've Done" and "What I Still Need to Do," respectively. He should then find a quiet place and spend a half-hour or so listing items on each of the sheets. What seems to be taken care of where your student's leadership skills and accomplishments are concerned? What does he still need to do? Encourage him to write it all down.

2. Advise your student to talk to other members of the organization as well as his faculty advisor (if the group has one). What do the group members and the advisor see as the leadership skills your student has already developed and the accomplishments he's already taken care of? And what do the group members and the advisor think your student still needs to work on where leadership skills and accomplishments are concerned?

3. Encourage your student to write down a few goals—some commitments about what he'll pursue in the coming months and how. Research has shown that written goals are much more likely than unwritten goals to become achieved goals!

4. Encourage your student to follow through on his commitments, and to remember to write down his challenges and successes as he goes along—because it will serve as great material for those job interviews he'll soon have!

• ROAD MAP QUESTIONS TO ASK YOUR STUDENT •

Passions: Is there anything you're passionate about improving in your campus organization? What kind of project or position really motivates you? Why?

Innate talents: What natural abilities and skills do you have that your campus organization could really use? How do you know? How can you use these strengths to make the organization stronger?

What matters most: Are your campus organization's activities genuinely important to you? Why or why not?

Internships and Co-op Experiences

Encourage your student to complete another internship or co-op experience, if possible (or her first one if she hasn't done one before).

Why

As we've noted throughout this *Parent Guide*, today's employers expect your student to come out of college with at least some hands-on experience in her chosen field. The more of that experience your student can accumulate through internships and co-ops, the better. It's easy for your student to have too little career-related experience when she graduates; it's impossible for her to have too much.

How

To learn about internship and co-op possibilities, your student can:

- Visit the campus career center (or its web site) and check out the internship and co-op listings it has obtained from specific organizations.

- Check out a college-oriented career web site like MonsterTRAK (*www.monstertrak.com*), Experience (*www.experience.com*), College Grad (*www.collegegrad.com*), or CollegeRecruiter (*www.collegerecruiter.com*) and look for internship and co-op listings there.

- Go to the campus library or a nearby bookstore and look through one of the many printed internship/co-op directories that are on the market (published by companies like Princeton Review and Peterson's).

- Talk to her professors and fellow students to see where current and previous students from her school/department have done internships or co-ops in the past.

- Talk to a counselor at the campus career center (particularly if the center has an *internship coordinator* or a similarly titled person on staff) to see where previous students from the school have interned or done co-ops in the past.

- Directly approach any organizations that interest her and ask (by phone or email) whether they have internship or co-op opportunities for college students.

• ROAD MAP QUESTIONS TO ASK YOUR STUDENT •

Passions: If you're doing another internship in the same field you interned in before, are you continuing to enjoy the industry and the work within that industry? Is your additional internship experience affirming your choice of field/industry?

Innate talents: Have you discovered that you're good at the work involved in this field/industry? Does your additional internship experience tell you anything new about your abilities and skills in relation to the field/industry—i.e., will you be successful in it?

What matters most: Does the additional internship experience you're obtaining tell you anything more about what working in this field/industry means to you? Will this line of work give you the type of life you want? Is it going to allow you to pursue whatever it is that's most important to you (e.g., achieving financial wealth, making a difference to society, tapping your creativity and independence)?

The Graduation Ceremony

Urge your student to participate in his graduation ceremony.

Why

Some college students decide not to participate in their school's graduation ceremony. Urge your student not to be one of them! Otherwise he'll miss out on a once-in-a-lifetime experience. He deserves to pick up that beautiful diploma he's been working so hard to obtain—and to be recognized, publicly, for his efforts.

How

1. At most schools, students have to officially apply for graduation—typically several weeks or even a few months before their expected graduation date (see p. 196). So encourage your student to check with his academic advisor or the Registrar's Office to see exactly what he needs to do, and when, to participate in the graduation ceremony.

2. Remind your student to order his cap and gown on time from the campus bookstore (or whatever campus department handles graduation caps and gowns).

3. If your student wants to, he can order some printed invitations to send out to family and friends who may want to attend his graduation. Be sure your student understands and observes the ordering deadlines established by the campus bookstore (or whatever campus department handles graduation invitations).

4. Urge your student to listen closely to what the graduation speaker has to say, take tons of pictures, and celebrate mightily afterwards. Congratulations! He's made it—and so have you!

• ROAD MAP QUESTIONS TO ASK YOUR STUDENT •

Passions: Have you really explored your passions during college? What would you do differently if you could?

Innate talents: Has the education you've received strengthened your innate talents? What experiences have benefited you the most over the past four years? What have those experiences given you where your future career is concerned—especially when it comes to new skills and expertise?

What matters most: Has your college experience helped you solidify what you want for your future—especially with respect to your career plans? What do you want, and why?

Focus on the Future

• CONTINUING TASKS •

- Encourage your student to continue developing his career portfolio (see p. 154) and to update it continuously.

- Encourage your student to continue researching careers in depth by not only reading about them, but also talking (in person or via phone/email) with people who actually work in them (*informational interviewing*—see p. 101). Urge your student to enhance his efforts by asking a campus reference librarian to show him how to obtain hard(er)-to-find information on companies/organizations that interest him.

- Advise your student to continue attending job/career fairs (see pps. 164 and 217)—on or off campus.

• NEW TASKS •

The Basic Cover Letter

Remind your student to write a basic cover letter she'll be able to send to prospective employers (or to graduate/professional schools, as the case may be).

Why

Your student can't send out a resume without an accompanying cover letter. Period. Prospective employers will look to your student's cover letter to:

- Learn about her very best traits, abilities, and achievements.
- Get an initial sense of her written communication skills.

They'll also look for evidence that your student has researched *their* particular organization and *their* particular job opening. Like all of us, employers have egos: They want your student to apply not just for any job in any organization, but *their* job in *their* organization.

How

1. Your student will need to start a new document in Microsoft Word (the most widely used word processing program, by far) and save it as "Basic Cover Letter." It's smart to include the date as part of the file name—e.g., "John Smith—Basic Cover Letter—10December2006."

2. On the top left-hand side of the page, your student should type her name and contact information (including address, phone number, and email address). This will obviously take several lines.

3. Next, she should hit the "Enter" key on her computer a couple of times to leave a little white space. She should then type today's date.

4. Now, your student should leave a little white space again and type the name and address of the person she's writing to.

5. Next, it's time for your student to begin her actual letter. Whenever possible, she should address the letter to a specific person—e.g., "Dear Ms. Johnson" or "Dear Dr. Evans." If she can't track down a specific name, she can use a generic phrase like "Dear Hiring Manager" or "Dear Recruiter."

6. The letter itself will be made up of three to five short paragraphs:

   - In the first paragraph, your student should describe why she's writing and how she learned of the position she's applying for. She should try to work in a brief mention of one or two of her key skills as well.

   - In the second and third paragraphs, your student should highlight any key traits, abilities and skills, or achievements she has that she believes the letter recipient will want to know about. (This is the place where she must outline the very best she has to offer.)

   - In the fourth paragraph, your student should ask to meet with the letter recipient to discuss the position in more detail (i.e., an interview). She should also stress the various ways the recipient can get in touch with her.

   - In the final paragraph, your student should thank the recipient for his/her time.

- Your student's letter should end with "Sincerely"—followed by three or four blank lines—then her name. (If she'll be sending her letter in print form, she should of course be sure to sign it first!)

7. Once your student has a first-draft cover letter completed, encourage her to set up an appointment with a campus career counselor for an evaluation of the letter.

8. At the meeting with the counselor, your student should take detailed notes on suggested changes and make them accordingly afterwards.

9. Advise your student that her cover letter needs to change slightly for each job (or school) she applies to. She'll need to customize her letter each time she uses it; a "one size fits all" letter usually fits none.

10. Proofread your student's cover letter if asked, and urge her to proofread her own letter each time she uses it.

• ROAD MAP QUESTIONS TO ASK YOUR STUDENT •

Passions: Does your excitement for this position—and your chosen field—come across in your cover letter? Will your letter set you apart from other candidates?

Innate talents: Do you have the writing skills necessary to land the job (or admission to the graduate/professional program) you're trying to pursue? Is your cover letter doing you justice?

What matters most: Does your cover letter show you'll be a good fit for the organization and its customers/clients? Do your values match those of the organization?

Revising the Resumé

Encourage your student to revise his resumé to reflect the experiences, skills, and accomplishments he gained during junior year and the summer following junior year.

Why

As you and your student know by now, a resumé is a living document that needs to change as your student grows professionally. It would be foolish for him to write his resumé once and then rest on it. After all, as he progresses through his college years, he gains more and more experiences, skills, and accomplishments to brag about.

How

1. Encourage your student to make an appointment with a campus career counselor for the purpose of revising his resumé.

2. Before the appointment, your student should take three sheets of paper—as he's done in years past—and label them "New Experiences," "New Skills," and "New Accomplishments," respectively.

3. Your student should take his "New Experiences" sheet and start jotting down any new experiences he can think of that have occurred between his junior year and now. Urge your student *not to limit himself at this point!* If something jumps into his mind—no matter how minor or insignificant it might seem—he should write it down. The idea is for your student to do a "brain dump" and get everything out of his head and onto paper. Later, he and his career counselor can decide what to add to the resumé and what to leave off.

4. Encourage your student to go through the same "brain dump" exercise with his "New Skills" and "New Accomplishments" sheets.

5. Once your student has finished writing down everything he can think of on each of these sheets, he should keep them in a handy spot … just in case he thinks of other entries to add later.

6. Encourage your student to bring the sheets to his appointment with the career counselor, and to ask for help remembering anything he may have forgotten or disregarded.

7. With the counselor's help, your student can decide which entries to add to his resumé and which to leave off. As usual, he'll almost certainly have to do some reformatting of the resumé to accommodate the changes.

8. Once your student has finished revising his resumé, remind him to ask the counselor to look at it one last time for minor revisions.

Passions: Do the activities listed on your resumé effectively illustrate your interests and passions?

Innate talents: Will employers (or graduate schools) be able to easily spot your top abilities and skills on your resumé? And will they see your *achievements*, not just your *activities/duties*?

What matters most: Does your finished resumé accurately represent you? Will it be your ticket into an interview for a position that is truly important to you?

Get a Second Opinion

Encourage your student to work closely with a campus career counselor or another expert (e.g., a knowledgeable professor, her internship and/or job supervisors and colleagues) to assess—and, if necessary, improve—the *strength* of her resumé and the *strength* of her cover letter.

Why

If, all by herself, your student writes the strongest resumé and the strongest cover letter possible—on the very first try—then she's a one-in-a-million case! In reality, none of us can develop a truly solid resumé or cover letter without a few additional sets of eyes—i.e., constructive feedback from other people.

If your student really wants her resumé and cover letter to be the best they can be, she'll readily acknowledge—and welcome—the ongoing suggestions she receives from knowledgeable people she can trust.

How

1. Once your student has a resumé and cover letter *she* is happy with, encourage her to start showing those documents to other people. For example, if she hasn't been working with a counselor at the campus career center, now is the time for her to see one so she can get some expert feedback on her documents. Remember: Your student is shooting not merely for *adequate* documents but *outstanding* ones!

2. Urge your student to seek other resumé and cover letter critiques as well—from favorite professors, internship or job supervisors and co-workers, members of any professional groups she's in, and friends/colleagues (hers and perhaps yours).

3. Encourage your student to carefully note the document feedback she receives from each person. She should keep in mind, however, that these documents are *hers*! She has final decision-making power over what feedback to use and what feedback to ignore.

4. Help your student use the feedback she receives (the feedback that seems good to her, that is!) to polish her resumé and cover letter one more time before she starts sending each of them out. Remind her, though, that she'll never truly be done with the revision process. Resumés and cover letters are living documents.

• ROAD MAP QUESTIONS TO ASK YOUR STUDENT •

Passions: Do your final resumé and cover letter accurately reflect what you're most passionate about? How do you know?

Innate talents: Will employers (or graduate schools) be able to easily spot your top abilities and skills on your final resumé? And will they see your *achievements*, not just your *activities/duties*? How do you know?

What matters most: Do the experiences you've highlighted on your resumé and in your cover letter reflect your values? Will employers view those values positively or negatively? How do you know?

Highlighting Abilities, Traits, and Accomplishments for Interviewing

Encourage your student to start jotting down stories from his past experiences that he can use in interviews to highlight his abilities, skills, traits, and achievements.

Why

Employers are savvy and skeptical. They've heard entry-level job applicants say things like "I have strong communication skills" and "I'm a good team player" hundreds of times. They've also been burned (often more than once) by job applicants who have made such claims in their interviews but demonstrated just the opposite once on the job.

In his interviews, your student will have to be ready to back up what he says about his abilities, skills, traits, and achievements. He can do that with brief stories from his past—from internships, classroom experiences, volunteering, and elsewhere—that serve as *evidence* of the abilities, skills, traits, and achievements he's claiming to have.

How

1. While your student will never know exactly what an employer is going to ask him about in a job interview, you can encourage him to make some educated guesses. Either on his own or, better yet, with the help of a campus career counselor, he should start listing the abilities, skills, traits, and achievements the employers in *his* chosen field will most likely seek in any candidate for an entry-level job. If, for example, your student plans to go into accounting, he can be sure a prospective employer will wonder about his ability to crunch complex numbers. If your student wants to go into social work, a prospective employer is no doubt going to ask him about his helping skills and experiences.

2. For each ability, skill, trait, or achievement he writes on his list, your student will need to think about one specific example from his previous experience that will show an employer he indeed possesses that ability, skill, trait, or achievement. Encourage him to use the following STAR acronym to write down his stories in detail:

- ST = **S**ituation you had to deal with, or **T**ask you had to perform
- A = **A**ction
- R = **R**esult

Suppose, for example, your student anticipates that a prospective employer will ask about his problem-solving skills. Here are some brief notes on a story he could tell to demonstrate those skills:

- ST = I was working with a group in my 400-level psych class and one of the people in my group wasn't pulling his weight on the major project we had to complete.

- A = I met him for lunch and asked him if there was something going on in his life that was preventing him from being more helpful to our group. Turns out his father was in the hospital, and so he was very distracted. So, with his permission, I went to the rest of the group and asked if each of them (me included) would be willing to take a small piece of his responsibilities so he could take an incomplete for the course and spend more time with his father.

- R = The group members quickly agreed to each take a part of the student's duties and we were able to move forward—without him losing face.

3. Remind your student to keep the notes about his stories in a file on his computer so that he can continually add to them. (This is not the time for him to scribble things down on pieces of scrap paper!)

• ROAD MAP QUESTIONS TO ASK YOUR STUDENT •

Passions: Do your stories illustrate what you're passionate about? How do you know you're being clear?

Innate talents: Do your stories reflect your strongest abilities and skills? How do you know?

What matters most: Will your stories help you answer interview questions in a way that will help the interviewer understand what's important to you?

Looking for Post-Graduation Job Opportunities

Encourage your student to start looking for post-graduation job opportunities.

Why

Now is the time for your student to start her post-graduation job search in earnest. It typically takes at least a few months for someone to find an entry-level job, and it can take longer if the economy and the job market are sluggish.

How

Here are ten specific ways your student can look for entry-level job possibilities. She can:

1. Visit the campus career center.

2. Network (see p 157). Encourage her to talk to people to either track down helpful contacts or learn about job openings that may not necessarily be widely advertised (or advertised at all).

3. Contact professional associations in her field. National, regional, and local professional groups exist in great part to help their members with their career development. As such, many organizations include field-specific job listings on their web sites or in their printed publications.

4. Visit company/organization web sites. Many companies and organizations post their job openings right on their own web sites (usually under an "Employment" or "Career Opportunities" or similarly titled section).

5. Apply directly to companies/organizations that interest her. Does your student want to work specifically for Company X or Organization Y? If so, encourage her to send a well-written cover letter and her resumé directly to the company, either to its human resources office or, often more effective, to the person who would likely make hiring decisions for the part of the organization that interests her.

6. Attend job/career fairs (see pps. 164 and 217). Many cities—particularly large ones—host job/career fairs, at various locations, throughout the year. Most colleges and universities hold their own job/career fairs as well, either individually or in collaboration with other institutions. A job/career fair is one of the few opportunities your student will ever have for employers *to come to her.*

7. Use college-specific web sites like MonsterTRAK (www.monstertrak.com), Experience (www.experience.com), CollegeRecruiter (www.collegerecruiter.com), and College Grad (www.collegegrad.com). These sites and others feature job listings geared specifically to college students and recent graduates. In most cases, your student can also upload her resumé into the databases the sites offer to prospective employers.

8. Use general web sites like Monster (www.monster.com), Career-Builder (www.careerbuilder.com), and HotJobs (www.hotjobs.com) as well as niche sites targeting her particular field. These sites feature job listings geared toward a more diverse group of job seekers. And, like their college-specific counterparts, most allow job seekers to upload resumés.

9. Use a placement agency. There are companies out there that specialize in helping people find jobs. Some of them even focus on working with college students and recent graduates. Maybe one of them can help your student. A word of caution, however: While most of these organizations receive their fees from *employers*, some will seek money from job seekers (i.e., your student). Warn your student to avoid any agencies that charge *job seekers*.

10. Consider temping. Often, by working as a *temp* (i.e., temporary employee) for a company for a short length of time, your student can position herself to be hired for a full-time, permanent position that opens up later on in the organization. Even if that doesn't happen, though, temping will help your student see various companies from the inside, meet people in her field of interest, and earn some decent money in most cases.

• ROAD MAP QUESTIONS TO ASK YOUR STUDENT •

Passions: Now that you're a senior—with much more knowledge, experience, and expertise than you had as a freshman—what settings/careers/industries appeal to you the most? What types of jobs do you want to pursue? Why?

Innate talents: In what settings/careers/industries will you most likely perform the best?

What matters most: Which settings/careers/industries will most likely allow you to live the kind of life you want to live?

Job/Career Fairs

Urge your student to attend job/career fairs, on and off campus.

Why

Going to a job/career fair is the most efficient and effective way for your student to meet a whole bunch of employers at the same time—employers who are in hiring mode to boot! It's a comparatively rare opportunity for your student to make many professional connections—in a very short period of time—with people who are ready to talk to him about job opportunities.

How

1. Encourage your student to stop by the campus career center (or visit its web site) to see what on- and off-campus job/career fairs are coming up over the next several months. Advise your student to watch the career section of his local newspaper as well, and to contact any local government or nonprofit career agencies in his area to see if they're aware of upcoming job/career fairs.

2. Encourage your student to determine which job/career fairs he'll be attending and to put them into his formal schedule or day planner.

3. Urge your student to think of each job/career fair experience in terms of what he should do *before*, *during*, and *after*:

Before

- Make sure your resumé is in solid shape. (If it isn't, ask a campus career counselor to help you improve it.) Print plenty of copies of your resumé when it's done so that you can hand it out to employers at the fair without fear of running out!

- Create some basic business cards. You can buy blank business cards at any office supply store and create your own finished cards in a word processing program. You can then print your cards on a laser printer or inkjet. No need to get super-fancy: Simply include your name, contact information, and perhaps your major and/or your broad career goals.

- Research the organizations that will be attending the fair. Visit their web sites to find out what they do. Make sure you're ready when an employer asks, "So, what do you know about us?"

- Spend a few minutes plotting—ahead of time—which employers you want to see at the job/career fair. Write down your top priorities, the next-most-important priorities, and so on. You want to use your time at the fair as efficiently as possible.

- Develop a thirty-second "commercial" describing who you are and what you offer. When an employer invariably says to you, "Tell me about yourself," you need to have something intelligent—and brief—to say to get the conversation going. So develop a thirty-second spiel ahead of time, and practice it with a friend or a campus career counselor so that it comes easily and naturally to you.

During
- When you arrive at the job/career fair—with many copies of your resumé in hand!—check in at the registration table, pick up any materials that are being handed out, and put on a name tag if one is offered.

- Pull out your list of top-priority companies/organizations and start visiting their tables. (Note: If you feel the need to warm up a bit, visit one of your lower-priority companies first!)

- Be prepared for introductions at each table and offer your hand for a handshake. Be sure your handshake is firm but not bone-breaking. (Note: Practice beforehand if you need to. It might seem silly, but your handshake is an important first impression of you.)

- Dress appropriately. This is not the time for shorts and flip-flops. At a minimum, dress *business casual*—maybe not suit-and-tie but certainly looking professional and presentable in nice-looking, cleaned-and-pressed clothes. If in doubt, *over*dress. (Note: It should go without saying that you'll want to be well groomed, too. And you may want to lose the nose ring for the day.)

- Ask good questions. Employers are impressed by job candidates who ask intelligent questions about the company, the job, the work environment, and the broader industry the company serves.

- Talk about what you *offer*, not what you *want*. You'll be a refreshing change of pace for the employer if you focus mostly on what you can do *for him/her*—instead of constantly asking about what the employer can do *for you*.

- Leave your resumé and business card with each employer you talk to.

After

- Immediately after the job/career fair, write detailed notes about who you visited with, what you discussed, and what you learned. You *won't* remember it all a week from now, when the names and faces of the various employers start to run together in your mind.

- Follow up on any promises you made. If you told an employer you'd send him/her something, do it. If you said you'd call or email, do it. If you don't, employers will likely perceive your lack of follow up as lack of caring—and promptly drop you from their A-list.

- Send or email a thank-you note to each employer you talked to at any length. It's common courtesy and, as importantly, it will make you stand out from the vast majority of the other job seekers who don't bother sending thank-you notes.

• ROAD MAP QUESTIONS TO ASK YOUR STUDENT •

Passions: Which companies/organizations at the job/career fair excite you the most, and why? Do they offer any particular products, services, or causes that truly tap your passions? Can you envision yourself having a blast working forty (or more) hours a week for a particular organization? Why?

Innate talents: Which of the companies/organizations would tap your best (and favorite) abilities and skills? What sorts of things could you do for these organizations? Where are your talents truly needed? How could you effectively market your talents to the organizations that could use them the most?

What matters most: Did you learn about any companies/organizations whose products, services, or causes match up with what's most important to you in life? Which of the companies/organizations could you really *believe in* at your core, and why? Conversely, which companies/organizations turned out to be real turnoffs for you, and why? Have you learned anything about what you *don't* want in your job or in the organization you work for?

Identifying Professional References

Encourage your student to identify three or four people who are willing to serve as *professional references* for her.

Why

Practically all prospective employers will want to talk to people—i.e., *professional references*—who know your student well and who can speak to her abilities, skills, traits, and experiences.

Sometimes employers will want to contact your student's references before bringing her in for an interview. Most often, though, they'll want to talk to her references *after* interviewing her—when they're almost (but not quite) ready to offer her the job. In either case, your student needs to have some people lined up who will speak highly of her.

How

1. Help your student think about people in her life who would be willing to serve as positive professional references for her. She can consider professors who know her well, advisors and/or counselors, internship/co-op/work supervisors, and others in positions of significant influence.

2. Advise your student to contact the people on her list and ask them if they'd be willing to be professional references for her. For each of the people who agree to be a reference, your student should prepare a brief list of the abilities, skills, traits, and accomplishments she hopes the person will be able to highlight (on her behalf) when that person talks to prospective employers. It's important for your student to help her references help her!

3. Your student should ask each of her references to write her a one- or two-page *letter of recommendation* that she can keep for future reference. While many employers these days will *not* take the time to read these letters, a few might. But either way, *your student* will have a written record of the insights each of her references provides on her behalf.

4. Encourage your student to prepare a printed list of her references, with full contact information for each. If—make that *when!*—an employer asks your student for her references, she can then send or email him/her the printed list.

5. Tell your student that she *must* alert each of her references when she has a feeling a particular employer may be contacting her references. Your student doesn't want her references to be caught off guard!

• ROAD MAP QUESTIONS TO ASK YOUR STUDENT •

Passions: Have you told your references what it is you dream about and why you're passionate about it? Do they know your ideal work setting? career? industry? Are you sure?

Innate talents: Have you asked your references what they think you're really good at? Do their assessments match your own? Have you shared with them how you've been developing your innate talents and building your skills?

What matters most: Do your references understand what truly motivates you? Do they know what's most important to you, especially in your future career?

Using the Career Portfolio

Encourage your student to work with a campus career counselor to learn how to use his *career portfolio* effectively in interviews.

Why

Last year, your student (hopefully!) created a *career portfolio* (see p. 154) using the many items he (hopefully!) began saving starting freshman year. (Note: If your student didn't create a career portfolio last year, now's the time.)

It's one thing for your student to *have* a career portfolio; it's quite another for him to know how to *use* his portfolio effectively—especially where it matters most: in interviews. A campus career counselor can help your student practice this key skill so that he'll confidently and competently present essential highlights from his portfolio in his interviews—in a way that doesn't overwhelm or, worse, turn off the person he's talking to.

Remember: Your student's portfolio is a tool that's intended to help him back up his claims in an interview situation. It's a presentation *tool*; it's not a presentation in and of itself. In other words, your student can't simply go into an interview, hand his portfolio to the employer, and sit back and watch. Instead, he needs to learn how to incorporate his portfolio into his overall presentation of himself. It's a little bit science and a lot of art—but your student can learn how to do it effectively if he's simply willing to practice ahead of time.

How

1. Encourage your student to set up a meeting with a campus career counselor so he can practice using his portfolio in an interview situation. (Note: If possible, your student should ask the counselor to videotape this practice session so he can review his performance afterward.)

2. With the career counselor's help, your student should work on the following activities as they relate to his use of a portfolio in an interview:

   • Alerting the employer that he has a portfolio.

   • Guiding the employer through his complete portfolio if he/she should ask. (Note: This is comparatively rare; most employers simply don't have the time or the desire to go through your student's entire portfolio, page by page. But it *does* happen, so your student needs to be ready for this possibility.)

   • Highlighting key pages in his portfolio based on specific questions an employer might ask. Example: "Tell me about a time when you led a team to accomplish something." Your student's possible response: Showing the employer the page in his portfolio featuring the letter he received from the president of his college, congratulating a team he led that raised a record amount of scholarship money for the school.

   • Figuring out what to do if the employer wants him to leave his portfolio behind. (Note: Generally, your student should *not* do this— unless he has a complete backup copy! But he can, for example, leave a mini-portfolio of key documents with the employer, or offer to make copies of key portfolio elements and leave them behind.)

3. Your student should also ask his career counselor if there are any parts of his portfolio that could be stronger and, if so, how he can improve them. If/when your student makes these improvements, he should practice presenting them to his career counselor in a follow-up session.

4. Encourage your student to set a goal of knowing his portfolio inside and out, backwards and forwards. He should be able to quickly turn to any particular page in his portfolio. He doesn't want to be stumbling and stalling in an interview situation! He'll be far more impressive to the employer when he can easily—and confidently—lead that employer through the key elements of his portfolio.

Passions: When you present your career portfolio (in whole or in part) to an interviewer, will he/she get a good idea of what your strongest interests are? If not, how can you address this problem?

Innate talents: Does your portfolio offer evidence that you have the abilities and skills you say you have, as well as the ones a particular employer is looking for? Do *you* do a good job of presenting the elements of your portfolio so that your key abilities and skills are crystal clear to the employer?

What matters most: When an employer looks at your portfolio, will he/she be able to easily spot what's important to you, especially where your career is concerned? And will you be able to effectively present these essential career values to the employer, using your portfolio as a visual backdrop?

Interviewing
Advise your student to interview for as many jobs as she reasonably can.

Why
For most people, interviewing is an odd and unnerving experience. But the more interviewing your student does, the better she'll be at it—and the more comfortable she'll become with the process.

Just as she didn't learn to ride a bike or play the guitar in a day or two, your student won't be outstanding at interviewing after a time or two (or three or four!). But as she goes through more interviews, she'll improve. And all the while, she'll increase her chances of landing a job.

How

1. Encourage your student to use the strategies outlined in the "Looking for Post-Graduation Job Opportunities" section (see p. 214) to pursue job leads. If—make that *when!*—an employer invites your student to interview for a position, encourage her to enthusiastically accept.

2. When the employer asks your student when she's available to interview, she should tell him/her she'll adjust her schedule to meet his/her needs. If it means skipping a class, so be it. Tell her there are times in life when she has to make a sacrifice for an important cause, and this is definitely one of those times! She wants to show that the employer's needs are important to her.

3. Once an interview is set up, remind your student to write down the day, time, and location—immediately—in her calendar. She doesn't want to have to call back later to be reminded of when her interview is (or *was!*).

4. Urge your student to prepare for the interview by researching the company/organization in considerable depth. Your student *must* be able to show the employer that she knows something about his/her organization. If she can't, the employer will conclude she's not serious about the job or the organization.

5. Either on her own or, better yet, with the help of a campus career counselor, your student should start thinking about the abilities, skills, traits, and achievements this employer is most likely to ask her about. Encourage your student to determine which of her STAR stories (see pps. 212-214) she'll tell in response to each question she thinks she'll be asked by her interviewer(s).

6. Encourage your student to practice telling her STAR stories to a friend or, even better, a campus career counselor. The friend/counselor should ask your student the questions she thinks she'll be asked in a real interview—using a *behavioral* format that requires your student to give examples to back up her claims. For example, instead of asking "How are your communication skills?" your student's friend/counselor can say, "Tell me about a time when you had to use good communication skills to solve a difficult problem."

7. On the day of her interview, your student should arrive five to ten minutes early. Advise her to be friendly and courteous to *everyone* she talks to, and to graciously accept coffee or water if it's offered.

8. After the interview is over, your student should thank her interviewer graciously and then—within twenty-four hours—send a thank-you note. In the note, your student should genuinely thank the interviewer(s) for his/her/their time, reiterate her interest in the job (assuming she *is* still interested!), and restate her key abilities and traits.

• ROAD MAP QUESTIONS TO ASK YOUR STUDENT •

Passions: Do your strongest interests align with the work of the organization you're interviewing with? Why or why not?

Innate talents: Will you be able to frequently use your strongest abilities and skills in the position you're applying for? How do you know? Will you struggle in the position or will you be successful? How do you know?

What matters most: Do you believe in the mission and vision of the organization you're interviewing with? Why or why not?

"Plan B"

Work with your student to develop a "Plan B" outlining what actions he'll take after graduation if he hasn't yet landed a job by that time.

Why

It's possible—especially if the economy and the job market are sluggish—that your student won't be able to land a job before he graduates from college. Don't panic! It's a frequent occurrence, and it's not a sign of your student's impending doom!

His best bet is to create a "Plan B"—actions he'll take to become the best job candidate he can possibly be. What's most important to employers is that he continue building his skills and acquiring new experiences during this time of transition. Employers will be impressed with how your student has spent his time if he's been creative, resourceful, and inventive.

How

1. Encourage your student to seek, if necessary, a pay-the-bills type of job that will allow him to stay afloat financially, yet still give him enough time to search for the post-graduation job he really wants.

2. If your student has been practicing networking strategies during his college years, now is the time for him to start re-contacting people he's gotten to know. Encourage him not to be afraid—or too proud—to ask for help. Remember: Your student isn't the only college graduate—present or past—who has been unable to land a job before graduation.

3. To the degree you can, help your student maintain a positive attitude. Encourage him to see this time of his life as a learning opportunity—one he'll probably never forget. The art of finding a job is a valuable skill that he'll use for the rest of his working life. By perfecting it now—by choice or by circumstance—your student will feel more confident during his future job transitions.

4. Urge your student to commit to daily activities that will keep him moving ahead in securing a job. Among the most important activities: networking, searching for jobs, sending out resumés and cover letters, following up on leads, writing thank-you notes, and conducting informational interviews. A job is not going to find your student; he'll have to find the job—and that involves *action*.

• ROAD MAP QUESTIONS TO ASK YOUR STUDENT •

Passions: What activity could you schedule each day to ensure your attitude stays positive? What do you love to do?

Innate talents: What are some ways you can use—and thus stay connected to—your favorite abilities and skills each day?

What matters most: Are you participating in *something* that matters deeply to you—even if it's a volunteer experience—so that you feel like you're still contributing to a cause or an organization that's truly important to you? If not, why not?

Post-Graduate Education

If applicable to her situation, encourage your student to begin researching graduate/professional schools and programs to see which ones interest her most.

Why

Your student will be investing a substantial amount of her time, energy, and money to attend graduate or professional school if she so chooses. So it's critical for her to find the program (and the school) that's the right fit for her—one that will help her achieve her career goals. Thorough research will help her do just that.

How

1. Encourage your student to start researching graduate/professional schools and programs in her fields of interest, either on her own or with the help of a campus career counselor. Some key resources she can use:

   - Print guides to graduate/professional schools (found in the campus career center or library or in any decent-sized bookstore). These guides are published by companies like Peterson's and Princeton Review.

   - Internet sites like Peterson's (www.petersons.com) and Princeton Review (www.princetonreview.com).

   - The web sites of specific schools and programs she's considering.

2. Encourage your student to collect information from the schools and programs that interest her the most. She should identify the ones for which she'll be academically eligible for acceptance by looking at their GPA requirements, their course or major requirements, and their minimum entrance exam scores.

3. Urge your student to talk to people who have firsthand experience with the programs and schools she's considering. It's important for your students to get a sense of what each program/school is like in the trenches, day to day.

4. As your student starts to narrow her choices down to two or three schools/programs, encourage her to contact the chairperson (or another faculty member) of each program's academic department and ask

questions. She should do the same thing with the graduate school/program admissions counselors for each school/program she's seriously considering.

• ROAD MAP QUESTIONS TO ASK YOUR STUDENT •

Passions: Do the graduate/professional schools and programs you're considering fit with your true passions? And how will obtaining a graduate degree from a particular school or program help you live your passions in a career?

Innate talents: Will the graduate/professional schools and programs you're considering strengthen your natural abilities and teach you essential new skills as well?

What matters most: Once you earn a graduate degree from a particular school/program, will you be able to pursue a career doing things that are really important to you?

Graduate/Professional School Entrance Exams

If applicable to his plans, encourage your student to take his graduate/professional school entrance exams (e.g., GRE, GMAT, LSAT, MCAT).

Why

Your student won't get into graduate/professional school without first jumping through the required hoops. The two main hoops are an entrance exam (required by many graduate/professional schools, though not all of them) and an application of some sort.

Urge your student to pay very close attention to the date of the entrance exam. He may want to allow himself enough time to take the test twice in case his first test scores don't reflect his best work. Remember, too, that it's always possible your student will get sick or run into bad weather the day of his entrance exam. So he should plan to take his entrance exam sooner versus later.

How

1. If your student knows he'll be going to graduate/professional school following graduation, encourage him to start working with his academic advisor and/or a campus career counselor early in his senior year in order to get ready.

2. With an advisor's/counselor's help, your student can figure out which graduate/professional school entrance exam(s) (if any) he'll need to take in order to be considered for graduate/professional school.

3. With an advisor's/counselor's help (if necessary), your student should obtain the application materials he'll need to complete so he can sign up to take his graduate/professional school entrance exam(s). (Note: Often, the campus career center or graduate school will have the various graduate/professional school entrance exam applications on hand. But your student can also obtain them directly from the various testing companies, right on their web sites.)

4. Encourage your student to complete the application materials immediately and send them in (with appropriate fees) well before the application deadline highlighted in the materials. A few (or several) weeks later, he'll be notified (by the testing company) about when and where he'll be taking his entrance exam.

5. Your student should consider preparing for his entrance exam by purchasing a self-study workbook from a local bookstore or taking one of the many preparation classes offered by the various testing companies.

6. If your student hasn't done so already, he should tell the company(ies) that administers his graduate/professional school entrance exam(s) where to send his results (i.e., which schools/programs he's applied to).

• ROAD MAP QUESTIONS TO ASK YOUR STUDENT •

Passions: Which parts of your entrance exam are you most excited to prepare for? Does your anticipation seem congruent with the topics you've enjoyed studying during your undergraduate years? How can you use this clue as you explore graduate/professional programs and schools?

Innate talents: As you prepare for your entrance exam(s), are you identifying which areas are your strongest? How? How will this knowledge help you the day of the exam? Conversely, which areas of the exam should you prepare for harder?

What matters most: Have you made it a priority to prepare for your graduate/professional school entrance exam(s), or have you left it to the last minute—or, worse, decided you won't prepare at all? What do these actions (or lack thereof) reveal about your feelings where attending graduate/professional school is concerned?

Applying for Graduate/Professional Schools

If applicable to her situation, encourage your student to complete and submit her graduate/professional school application well before the deadline specified by the school/program she's applying to.

Why

One of the easiest (and most common) ways for your student to take herself out of the running for the graduate/professional program she's applying to is to miss the application deadline. So urge your student to send her application in early!

Many graduate/professional school applications are due in late November or early December. So your student needs to plan ahead to ensure she submits all the pieces of her application on time. She'll likely need the following items, at a minimum:

- The graduate/professional school application itself.
- Her graduate/professional school entrance exam scores.
- Her reference letters.
- Her personal statement.
- Her academic transcripts.
- Evidence of certain experience (depending on the program/school). If your student is applying to a physical therapy program, for instance, that program may require her to have a certain number of volunteer hours in a related area.

How

1. Encourage your student to obtain applications from the graduate/professional schools and programs she'd like to apply to. (Note: These days, your student can usually get the materials she needs from the institution's web site, but on occasion she may have to call/email and have the materials sent.)

2. Remind your student to fill out her application materials carefully, completely, and neatly.

3. If your student needs to prepare an application essay or *personal statement* (see p. 232) of some sort, encourage her to work closely with her academic advisor or a campus career counselor to write a draft, revise, write another draft, revise again, and write the final draft.

4. Urge your student to submit her completed application well before the deadline established by the school or program.

5. Encourage your student to prepare for the possibility that she'll have to interview (in person) with professors at one or more of the schools she's applied to. (Note: She can prepare for these interviews in much the same way she'd prepare for a job interview—see pps. 212-214.)

• ROAD MAP QUESTIONS TO ASK YOUR STUDENT •

Passions: Does your excitement for the discipline you hope to study come across in your graduate/professional school application? Will you stand out from the crowd?

Innate talents: Have you highlighted on your application your strongest abilities and skills? Will the admissions decision makers be able to see what you'll bring to their particular program?

What matters most: Do your application materials—especially any essays you've written—effectively illustrate why it's so important for you to further your education in the discipline you hope to study? How do you know?

The Personal Statement

Help your student write a compelling *personal statement* to accompany his graduate/professional school application.

Why

The *personal statement* serves as your student's "voice" in the initial graduate/professional school admission process. It introduces him to the selection committee and describes his most relevant experiences and what he's learned from them.

So your student must write a compelling, grammatically sound statement that represents *him*.

How

1. Each of your student's graduate/professional school applications will require its own approach to developing a personal statement and answering any essay questions your student is asked. So urge your student to read the questions carefully and answer them clearly. This advice might sound terribly obvious on the surface. But one of the biggest mistakes graduate/professional school applicants make is trying to use the same statement for each school they apply to instead of tweaking each one to address each school's/program's specific questions. It's typically very obvious to the selection committee who has taken the time to think about the school's/program's specific questions and who has not.

2. Urge your student to give himself plenty of time to write his personal statement and answer any essay questions he's asked. This process will take a while and will require some rewrites.

3. Encourage your student to show his personal statement to his academic advisor, faculty members who know him well, and others who can give him expert feedback on it. Do they think the statement is compelling? And do they think your student's responses to the essay questions represent him accurately and positively?

• ROAD MAP QUESTIONS TO ASK YOUR STUDENT •

Passions: Does your passion for the academic work you'll be doing come across effectively in your personal statement? How do you know? Have you clearly told the selection committee what you want to do with your graduate/professional degree and why?

Innate talents: Have you effectively highlighted the best you have to offer—your strongest abilities and skills—in your personal statement? How do you know?

What matters most: Will the selection committee get to know the real you through your personal statement?

Visiting Graduate/Professional School Campuses

Encourage your student to visit the campuses and interview professors and students at each to learn more about her top graduate/professional school choices.

Why

Choosing a graduate/professional school is a process that's similar to the one your student probably went through when she chose her undergraduate institution. The stakes, however, are considerably higher.

Your student must find a program that matches her interests, her learning style, and her values. She needs to figure out whether she connects with the faculty at a particular school and whether she feels comfortable there (especially since she'll be there several years!). Your student also needs to determine whether she feels at home in the various communities she'll potentially be a part of—the community within her prospective academic department, the larger institutional community, and the surrounding local community.

How

1. Visiting campuses and interviewing people at those schools is a two-way process—your student is judging and being judged. First impressions count. So remind your student to be professional during the

entire visiting and interviewing process, from how she contacts the program to set up the visit to what she wears the day she arrives.

2. Encourage your student to prepare for her visits/interviews in two ways. First, just as she would for a job interview, she should use the STAR technique (see pps. 212-214) to prepare stories illustrating her best abilities, skills, and experiences. Attending graduate/professional school is the "job" she wants. Second, she should prepare (and write down) questions of her own to ask the professors, students, and staff members she meets during her visits.

3. Your student should make sure each of her visits is comprehensive. She should talk to faculty members and students; sit in on a class (or two or three); look at possible living arrangements; find out about research assistantships, fellowships, teaching assistantships, and scholarships; and visit with financial aid personnel.

4. Some graduate/professional school programs have very strict visit policies, so your student may not have much control over her visit. If that's the case, encourage her to do the best she can to get her questions answered informally. She may need to rely on speaking to alumni/ae of the program to get her best information.

5. Remind your student to collect contact information from everyone she meets on campus so she can follow up with a thank-you note to each person immediately after she gets home. It's common courtesy to thank people for their time and insights—and your student will stand out in doing so.

• ROAD MAP QUESTIONS TO ASK YOUR STUDENT •

Passions: Are you ready to speak succinctly about why a particular graduate/professional school and program are a good fit for you? How do you know?

Innate talents: As you look around a particular campus and talk to various people there, do you think you'll be able to use your favorite abilities and skills—and learn new ones—during your time at the institution?

What matters most: Can you see yourself pursuing your dreams at a particular school you've visited? Could it be your next home? How do you know?

*dreams … discoveries … reflections …
intentions … discussions*

Mapping Your Direction

Uncovering Your Purpose
Senior Year

*"What is happiness: to be dissolved into
something complete and great."*

~ WILLA CATHER

Your student is standing at the door to an incredible and exciting transition—his post-college life! How will he greet this transition and his changing world? What mark does he want to leave on the world in the years to come? What is his purpose and how will he live his life with that purpose?

These are the questions your student should ponder as he completes his senior year. If he can answer even a few of these questions, he'll go into the The Real World with confidence and competence.

Purpose

Encourage your student to answer the following questions so she can continue to delve deeper into her purpose and reach her dreams.

How do you want to go into the world now that your undergraduate education will soon be complete? In what areas do you have complete confidence? What can you rely on in difficult times? What are your gifts?

Dreams—Life's Destinations

Senior year is difficult because your student is trying to stay in the present, yet think about his post-graduation future at the same time. Encourage him to consider the questions that follow to put everything in useful context.

Where do you want to go at the end of your senior year? Do you want to live with a roommate, travel abroad, start a job, move home for a while? What will speak to the very core of your being as a young adult? How can you focus on the positive aspects of your upcoming transition and keep your mind from becoming fearful?

Discoveries

Your student will need to have a true understanding of what excites her now and what has been good along her path in college so she can continue on a positive path beyond her undergraduate years. She'll need this wisdom when the road gets bumpy.

Scenic highways: What makes you feel totally alive and filled with excitement? As you leave this year behind, what do you want to take with you that has been a tremendously positive part of your life?

_____

_____

_____

_____

_____

_____

Roadblocks and speed bumps: What are you scared of or apprehensive about as you move out of your undergraduate years at college? How will you face these fears?

_____

_____

_____

_____

_____

_____

_____

Reflections

Encourage your student to understand and appreciate his own uniqueness. If he's reflected along the way, he will have a real connection with what makes him special.

Have you discovered your own wisdom? Take at least ten minutes to write freely about what you have to offer the world with your personality, innate talents, skills, passions, and values. What makes you unique?

_____

_____

_____

_____

_____

_____

_____

_____

_____

_____

_____

_____

_____

_____

_____

_____

_____

Intentions

Encourage your student to set intentions so that he moves ahead in the direction he wants.

Set your course: How will you examine your post-college world to make sure that what matters most to you is a central theme of your life? How will you live in the world that awaits you? Will you be reflective? open to learning? confident? quiet? observant? How will these intentions help you in being true to yourself?

_____

_____

_____

_____

_____

_____

Daily intentions: What activities can you pursue each day of your senior year to best position yourself for your post-college life? How can you boost your confidence and reduce any apprehension you might have? Who can you turn to for help with these important tasks?

_____

_____

_____

_____

_____

_____

_____

Discussion and Dialogue

Now is a time when your student should take stock of her relationship with you and acknowledge how it has changed as she has emerged into a soon-to-be college graduate.

Assessing your support system: Over these last few years, how has your relationship changed with the people who make up your support system?

Mapping Your Direction

As your student leaves college, he'll need to forge a new direction for his future. Encourage him to seek a future he's excited about—one that connects him with the deeper sense of who he is and what he offers the world as an educated human being. The following questions will help.

Evaluate your senses, thoughts, feelings, and intuition right now. Do you have more clarity? What's still confusing to you? How can you cultivate and then maintain a healthy self-confidence? What do you need to do to get where you want to go?

The Best Is Yet to Come

Congratulations! Your student has graduated from college—an achievement you've likely looked forward to with much anticipation. But as you've probably realized, your student—make that *graduate!*—will need your support through the often complicated transition to the world of work.

Fascinating times lie ahead as your new grad leaves college for a future full of possibilities. By using *The College to Career Road Map* as a compass, she has established a foundation for living a life full of purpose. Her world is ripe with opportunity. Even more exciting, you know your new grad is now equipped with the skills she needs to make wise choices—because she's already practiced how to make life decisions from the "inside out."

Your new grad will be making career choices based on what she's passionate about, how she can best utilize her innate talents, and what matters most to her. The process of experiencing and reflecting outlined in *The College to Career Road Map* has helped her find her internal compass. She can now continue to practice this process as she makes her way through life and follows the direction she knows is best for her.

As a parent, you can continue to support your new grad by simply being available to listen to her life stories as they unfold, and by posing questions that support the reflective process as she continues to uncover her purpose.

We at College to Career, Inc. (www.collegetocareer.net) wish your new grad well on her journey to reach her potential and fulfill her purpose. The possibilities are endless!

Kind regards!

Terese, Peter, and Judy

About the Authors

Terese Corey Blanck, M.Ed., offers unique expertise in college student development combined with in-depth knowledge of post-college business employment needs. For the past twenty years, Terese has worked closely with college students and recent graduates, helping them identify their innate talents and desires, plan their educational and career paths, and enhance both their personal development and career employability.

After receiving her Bachelor of Science degree in Elementary Education from Minnesota State University–Mankato and her Master of Education degree in College Student Development from Colorado State University, Terese spent the next twelve years working for small private universities as well as large public universities in the area of student affairs. She then joined the private sector, coaching college students and recent grads in career and life exploration.

Terese was inspired to launch College to Career, Inc. when she opened and managed the Minneapolis office of Grad Staff, Inc., a specialty-niche staffing firm that matched recent college graduates with employers such as Target, Wells Fargo Bank, and Best Buy. Through this work, she discovered that many recent graduates leave college not knowing what they want to do, much less having prepared themselves for the world of work. In response to this unmet and critical need, Terese founded College to Career, Inc. to offer students a means for making decisions with direction during college—so they succeed after college.

A frequent speaker on college campuses, Terese also presents at major conferences on the topic of college student development. She has published numerous articles in the general market and lives in Minnesota with her husband and daughter.

Peter Vogt, M.S., is a career counselor, author, and speaker who encourages young adults to explore their many career possibilities and challenge the limiting beliefs, assumptions, and perceptions they often have about themselves and the world of work.

Peter devotes most of his time to writing and presenting for college students, college parents, and career practitioners across the United States. He's The MonsterTRAK Career Coach for leading global career web site Monster (www.monster.com); publisher of *Campus Career Counselor* (www.campuscareercounselor.com), a national newsletter for college/university career services professionals; and author of the book *Career Wisdom for College Students* (Facts On File, 2007). He's also been interviewed for articles in *Time* magazine, *U.S. News & World Report*, *The New York Times*, and many other media outlets.

Peter holds a master's degree in counseling from the University of Wisconsin–Whitewater and a bachelor's degree in mass communications from Minnesota State University–Moorhead. He lives in Minnesota with his wife and son.

Judith Anderson, M.A., has acquired a unique perspective working with college students and their parents at both large and small institutions throughout her entire professional career.

For the past twelve years, Judith has worked on college campuses in various roles in admissions, orientation and first-year programs, student leadership development, mentor programs, career services, residence life, and alumni relations. She has advised students in various student leadership roles, helping them discern and develop their innate talents, interests, and skills. Serving in these roles, she saw not only the importance of academic preparation, but more importantly experience, passion, and clarity for one's future endeavors.

Judith received her Bachelor of Arts degree in Political Science and Speech Communication from the University of Minnesota and holds a master's degree in Student Development in Higher Education from the University of Iowa. Most recently, she has served as a higher education consultant working both on campus and in the private sector. She has co-authored two handbooks for faculty members teaching first-year students at the University of Minnesota. As a partner with College to Career, Inc., Judy brings her campus experience and knowledge to parents and students, helping them make the most of their college experience. She lives in Minnesota with her husband and three children.

Judy Anderson, Peter Vogt, and Terese Corey Blanck